Short and Simple Guide To Smart Investing

Short and Simple Guide To Smart Investing

Alan Lavine
and
Gail Liberman

Authors Choice Press
New York   Lincoln   Shanghai

To: Ina and Monroe, Jack and
in memory of Esther.

Short and Simple Guide to Smart Investing

Authors Choice Press
an imprint of iUniverse, Inc.

For information address:
iUniverse, Inc.
2021 Pine Lake Road, Suite 100
Lincoln, NE 68512
www.iuniverse.com

Originally published by John Wiley & Sons

ISBN: 0-595-26892-7

Printed in the United States of America

Contents

Acknowledgments

The author would like to thank Wendy Grau, a former editor at John Wiley & Sons, for her help in making this book possible.

I would also like to thank my editors Mary Schroeder, editor of *Financial Services Week*; Bill Castle, business editor at the *Boston Herald*; Tom Siedell and John Wasik, senior editors at *Your Money* and *Consumers Digest*. Also special thanks to Lenny Greenberg for his assistance in researching information on specific companies mentioned in the book.

Portions of this book have appeared in *Your Money* and *Consumers Digest* magazines.

PART 1

THE BASICS

CHAPTER 1

Overview of Mutual Fund Investing

I f you lack the time and expertise to manage your
investments, consider mutual funds. Mutual
funds represent a pool of investors' money that's
managed by an investment professional.

That's why thousands of Americans have turned
to mutual funds as a way to save and invest. According to the Investment Company Institute, an industry trade group, one out of four families invests
in mutual funds. There are almost 100 million shareholder accounts in mutual funds. In 1940, there were
just 300,000 accounts invested in 68 funds with about
$500 million in assets. Today there are more than
3,000 mutual funds on the market with over $1.4
trillion in assets and 60 million shareholders. Figure
1.1 graphically tracks mutual fund growth.

Mutual funds are popular because they make it
easy for the average person to invest. A mutual
fund takes an investor's money and buys securities
based on the investment objectives of the fund.
The funds invest in stocks, bonds, money market
instruments such as certificates of deposit (CDs),
and other kinds of assets. The minimum initial and
subsequent investment requirements are low because a lot of people put money in the fund. You

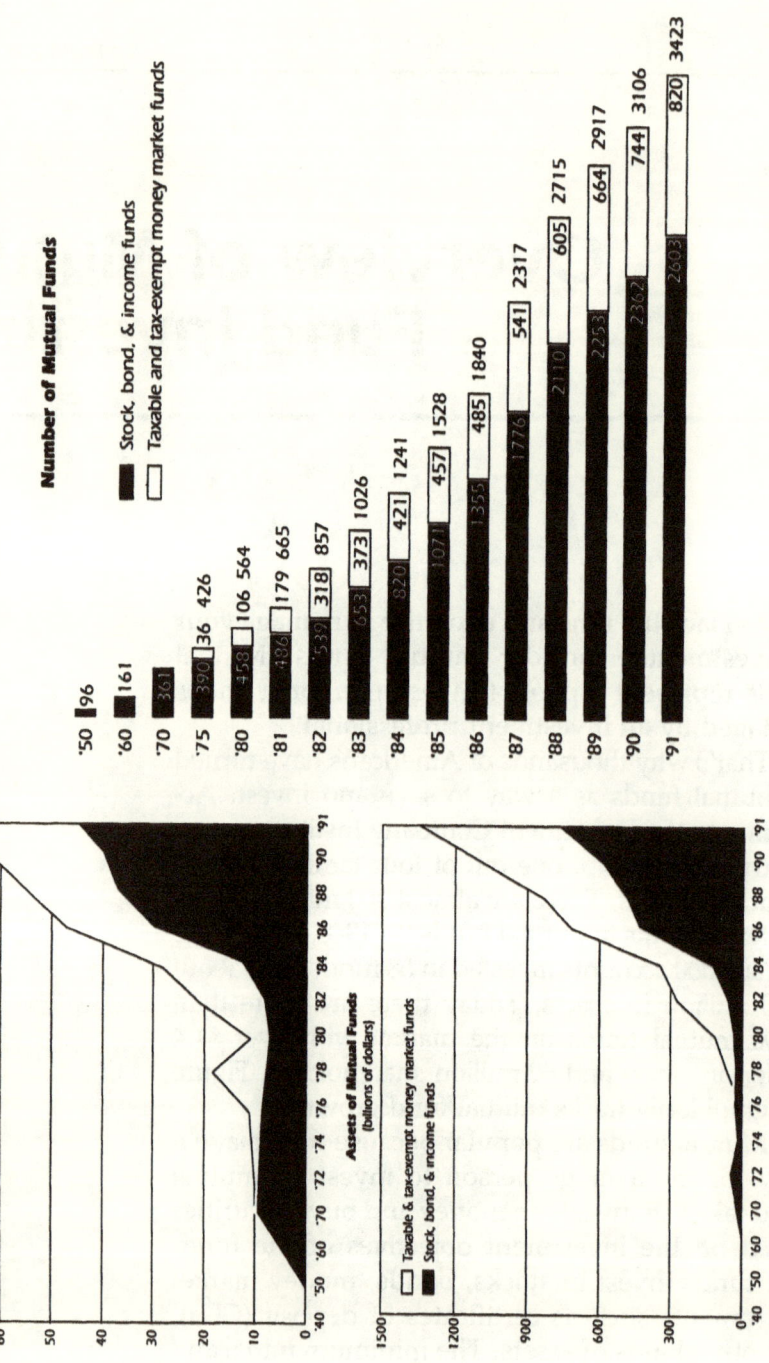

Figure 1.1. Mutual fund growth.

4

can invest as little as $1 in a few funds. Most funds require initial investments of $1,000.

The securities purchased by the fund make up the portfolio. The fund may receive income from interest payments and *dividends* or earn *capital gains* on the sale of a security at a profit. The fund distributes the earnings to the investors as dividends or capital gains. Or, upon your request, the fund will reinvest the earnings and buy you more shares.

Dividends and capital gains are paid out to shareholders in proportion to the number of fund shares they own. Shareholders who invest a few hundred dollars get the same investment return per dollar as those who invest hundreds of thousands of dollars.

GOOD RETURNS MAKE 'EM ATTRACTIVE

Financial advisers aren't surprised by the growth in mutual fund investing. Michael Lipper, a leading authority on mutual funds and president of Lipper Analytical Services in New York, believes that the growth of the U.S. economy over the past decade and the simplicity of mutual fund investing contribute to the interest in mutual funds.

"You get professional management and diversification," says Lipper. "Over the past 15 years the average equity income fund has grown at an annual rate of 14.72 percent and bond funds have gained 9.41 percent. That's an incredible return for the average investor. You won't likely see those types of returns in the future, but investors will get long-term growth over inflation."

FLYING FIRST CLASS AT COACH FARES

Although you can invest in individual securities, experts say most people can't afford it. You need

dividend: short-term profits, stock dividends, or interest income distributed by mutual funds to shareholders in the form of cash or more shares

capital gains: the profit made when a fund manager sells securities in the portfolio; also the profit realized by the shareholder when fund shares are sold (When a fund realizes capital gains, the gains are distributed to the shareholders of the fund either in cash or reinvestment of new shares.)

about $100,000 to diversify your portfolio properly. Because many people don't have that much money and lack the time to do the right kind of research, experts say they should stick with mutual funds for the following reasons.

Investment Pros Do the Driving

Mutual funds represent a professionally managed, diversified portfolio of stocks and bonds or a combination of both. Many funds have in-house analysts and research staffs who review financial and economic data and select securities that represent the best value for capital appreciation or income. In addition, many mutual fund companies offer financial incentives to their portfolio managers who outperform the general market.

Lower Risk through Management

A diversified portfolio of stocks or bonds reduces risk. Financial research published in the *Journal of Business* as far back as 1966 has shown, for example, that 60 percent of the time a stock's price moves in tandem with the overall market. That is known as market risk. Another 20 to 30 percent of a security's price is determined by specific information about a company and/or its industry's outlook. Lady Luck is the remaining factor that can influence a stock's price.

diversification: splitting your investments among different types of mutual funds to reduce risk, or choosing mutual funds that hold a large number of issuers in a wide variety of industries

With mutual funds, however, you can cut your risks. A fund with a large number of stocks will not get hurt if one or two companies fall on bad times and their stock prices tumble. If you own a mutual fund that holds a large number of issues, your losses are cushioned if one stock plunges because of bad news or unfavorable analyst comments.

Here is how *diversification* works to protect you.

Assume you own 100 shares of the following: Citi-Corp, which you purchased at $22 per share; IBM, at $104; Phelps Dodge, at $53; and Commonwealth Edison, at $32.

You spent $21,000 assembling this portfolio, and your average share price is $52.75. Six months later, you check the stock listings in the newspaper and are happy to find that your stocks are up. Citi-Corp is up to $25. IBM is at $121. Phelps Dodge is down to $48, and Commonwealth Edison is trading at $31.

The market value of your Phelps Dodge and Commonwealth Edison stocks declined $500 and $100, respectively. But the value of your CitiCorp and IBM stocks more than covered your losses, increasing by $300 and $1,700, respectively.

The rule of thumb is that the greater the number of stocks in a portfolio, the lower the portfolio's risk. In other words, the greater the number of stocks in your mutual fund, the less likely it is that you will see wide swings in the market value of the fund.

Diversification helps to reduce the risk of losses if some stocks in the portfolio decline in value. But you have to remember that all stocks tend to move in the same direction as the overall stock market about 60 percent to 70 percent of the time according to financial research. You always face market risk when you invest in mutual funds. In other words, the entire portfolio will, in part, move in the same direction as the entire market for stocks.

Fortunately, there is a way to reduce market risk. If you diversify your mutual fund holdings, for example, in stocks, bonds, money funds, precious metals, and overseas mutual funds, you can reduce risk of loss when the stock market here at home declines. Other assets don't perform in tandem with the U.S. stock market. So losses in stocks could be offset by gains in international stock or bond funds or a rally in the precious metals market.

Here's how diversification among mutual funds really works: On October 26, 1987, the Dow Jones Industrial Average lost a whopping 8 percent when the stock market crashed. But a portfolio that included 15 percent blue-chip stocks, 15 percent over-the-counter growth stocks, 15 percent overseas stocks, 15 percent U.S. bonds, 20 percent overseas bonds, 5 percent gold, and 15 percent in money market funds declined just 3.8 percent.

Chapter 3 discusses the risks and rewards of stock and bond fund investing in detail. For now, it's important to note that you can't eliminate market risk or risk due to bad news about a company, but you can cut your losses by investing in a mutual fund that owns a large number of securities, and by investing in different types of mutual funds.

no-load mutual fund: a fund free of sales charges

load: a sales charge that can range from 2 percent to 8.5 percent; may be paid at time of purchase (front-end load) or when fund is sold (back-end load)

contingent deferred sales charge: a back-end redemption charge that declines to zero over a specified number of years, after which fund shares can be sold without paying a back-end load

Good Performance

Mutual funds give you good long-term performance. Financial research shows that over decades all investments will experience ups and downs in performance. From 1926 through 1992, financial assets have experienced large gains. According to data published by Ibbotson & Associates in Chicago, the Standard & Poor (S&P) 500 Stock index earned an annual compound rate of return of 10.3 percent.

Long-term corporate bonds averaged 5.4 percent, long-term government bonds averaged 4.9 percent, and U.S. Treasury bills averaged 3.7 percent.

Liquidity

Mutual funds offer investors liquidity. The majority of investment companies have a stable of mutual funds with different investment objectives to pick from. Investors have the ability to make a telephone call to the fund and switch out of their existing fund into other funds as their financial needs or investment conditions change. For example, in 1982, when interest rates started to decline from their double-digit levels, money flowed out of money funds into equity funds as the bull market was launched. Investors also have liquidity because they can redeem fund shares by telephone or move into a money fund that offers check-writing privileges.

Low Fees

Mutual funds are also a low-cost way to invest in the financial markets. You can invest for as little as $200 to $1,000 and make subsequent investments of just $50 into your favorite mutual fund. Many funds have no sales charges; these are called *no-load mutual funds*. If you do pay a *load*, it can range from as little as 2 percent to as much as 8.5 percent and may be charged up front or when the fund is sold. Management fees for running the portfolio are usually 0.5 percent or less, depending on the total assets in the fund. Several fund groups have *contingent deferred sales charges* ranging from 1 percent to 6 percent, depending on when shares are redeemed. And some funds charge you *12b-1* or *sales distribution fees* that range from 0.25 percent to 1 percent annually.

Automatic Investment and Withdrawal

Mutual funds also enable you to make *automatic investments* and *systematic withdrawals*. By checking the appropriate box on the application form, you can set it up so that money can be electronically taken out of your checking account and invested

12b-1 fees: marketing distribution fees, ranging from 0.25 percent to 0.5 percent of assets, that shareholders pay annually

sales distribution fees: annual fees that can range from 0.25 percent to 1 percent of total assets in fund and are used to pay for promotion and distribution of fund shares (also known as a 12b-1 fees)

automatic investments: process of electronically debiting your checking account and automatically investing the money in the fund of your choice

systematic withdrawals: a fixed percentage of fund assets paid out to investors who primarily want additional income in your fund. Some funds have contractual plans whereby you agree to invest a regular amount for a specific time period. You can also instruct the fund to automatically withdraw a percentage of your account every month. This systematic withdrawal privilege is frequently used by retired people who live on fixed incomes. For example, as a retiree, you may elect to have 4 percent of a fund paid out to you each year to supplement your retirement income.

High Regulation

Mutual funds are one of the most highly government regulated investment vehicles you can purchase. You don't have to worry about being cheated out of your money when you invest in mutual funds. You get all the information you need in a mutual fund's prospectus. All mutual funds are required by law to display the same set of information in the fund's prospectus.

Securities and Exchange Commission: the U.S. government agency that regulates mutual fund or investment companies under the Investment Company Act of 1940

"The laws governing mutual funds require exhaustive disclosure to the *Securities and Exchange Commission*, state regulators, and fund shareholders, says Eric Kantor, spokesperson for the Investment Company Institute in Washington, DC. "The laws also entail continuous regulation of fund operations."

There are four major federal laws regulating mutual funds that serve to protect you from fraud and deceptive practices. The laws, however, don't protect you from poor investment decisions. So if you invest in a high-risk stock fund and you are aware that the investment is risky, then you have no recourse in a court of law.

Laws Regulating Mutual Funds

1. Securities Act of 1933. This act requires investment companies to register their funds with the

Securities and Exchange Commission. The registration statement contains important information about the fund. Investment companies are also required to provide interested investors with a prospectus. The prospectus contains in-depth information about how the fund is managed, investment policies, objectives, and other data.

2. Securities Exchange Act of 1934. This act protects investors against fraud. Institutions and people who sell mutual funds are regulated by both the Securities and Exchange Commission (SEC) and the National Association of Securities Dealers, a self-regulatory organization.

3. Investment Advisers Act of 1940. Investment advisers are required to file annual information about their finances and investment activities to the SEC.

4. Investment Company Act of 1940. This act prohibits self-dealing by those who work for the mutual fund company. Fund officers also must carry fidelity bond coverage if they have access to the investment company's securities. The act places limits on fees and commissions that shareholders may pay.

Bankruptcy is not a concern either. Your mutual fund assets can go up and down in price, but losses can't be more than the assets.

But what happens if the fund's sponsor, underwriter, or investment adviser is experiencing financial problems? You don't have to worry. Their creditors don't have access to your money. Your mutual fund, by law, is a separate company. You are the shareholder. As Elaine Kostikos, spokesperson for Founders Asset Management in Denver, says, "Stringent regulatory safeguards protect mutual fund shareholders from being affected by any potential difficulties of the mutual fund adviser or other companies affiliated with the fund manager."

Under the Investment Company Act of 1940, a mutual fund must adhere to rules governing the custody of shareholders' securities. Most mutual funds use bank custodians. The law requires custodians to put the fund's assets in an account separate from other assets. The custodian cannot deliver cash or securities from that account unless it receives proper instructions from the officers of the mutual fund. The shareholders have to give the mutual fund instructions before the officers can invest or redeem shares.

A FUND FOR ALL SEASONS

Mutual funds come in different varieties based on risk and investment objectives. With more than 4,000 mutual funds on the market, some say there's a mutual fund for all seasons. This enables individuals to match their level of risk and investment goals with the mutual fund's objectives. While no two mutual funds are exactly alike, they fall into several broad-based categories.

capital appreciation: the profit made on an investment, i.e., the increase in the value of the fund shares over time

Aggressive growth funds. These are the riskiest type of equity funds. These funds seek maximum *capital appreciation* and provide little current income to investors. Typically the funds invest in new companies or existing growth companies that are traded on the over-the-counter stock market. The funds may also invest in companies or industries that are out of favor, regardless of capitalization, because of the profit potential in undervalued or overlooked stocks. Other aggressive growth funds will invest in any size company that shows strong profit potential.

In the 1960s, aggressive stock funds were called "go-go" funds. Today, things haven't changed. These funds have the ability to outperform the market by as much as 25 percent to 30 percent. On the downside, however, investors can lose just as much, if the portfolio manager's stock selection is wrong or the overall market is in a steep decline.

Look, for example, at the Alliance Quasar Fund. This fund invests in small-company stocks that are considered undervalued, but the companies are leaders in their industries and should exhibit strong earnings growth. Over the past 15 years, ending in 1990, the fund has grown at an annual rate of 19.85 percent. But that return masks some volatile years. In 1984, for example, the fund lost 10.3 percent; and by the end of August 1990, the fund was down 18.13 percent. But in 1988 and 1989, the fund gained 29.73 percent and 28.30 percent, respectively.

Aggressive stock funds are riskier than other types of stock funds. That's why financial advisers say you should only have a small portion of your portfolio in aggressive funds.

Small-company stock funds. These funds are also high risk. Unlike aggressive stock funds, however, the portfolio managers invest only in small companies that trade on the over-the-counter market. The stocks are thinly traded and highly volatile. You can get some whopping returns over the short term, but you can also lose as much as a third of your money if the market moves the wrong way.

Growth funds. Like their aggressive cousins, growth funds look for capital appreciation. They are, however, less risky because the funds invest in well-seasoned companies that also pay dividends. Income from a growth fund is a secondary consideration. For example, Janus Fund, up 18.5 percent annually over the past 15 years ending in 1990, currently yields just 1.2 percent. But the fund owns such blue-chip stocks as Merck, American Express, and Boeing. For growth, it has a stake in fast-growing companies like Wal-Mart, a retailer, and MCI Communications, an over-the-counter telephone company.

Growth funds run neck and neck with aggressive stock funds in the performance ratings. On average, the funds have grown at an annual rate of 15 percent over the past 15 years, 12 percent over the past 10 years, and 9 percent over the past 5 years. They have slightly outpaced aggressive funds over the past 5 and 10 years.

For that reason, advisers recommend that you keep a stake in growth stock funds if you want a long-term investment that is less volatile than a go-go fund. Lipper recommends that investors of all ages stash some cash in growth stock funds. Regardless of your age, he says, "You should keep the bulk of your investment in stock funds." Investors, he adds, should assess their risk tolerance and keep a hand in the stock market.

"People of retirement age still have a long life expectancy," Lipper notes. "Some at age 60 could have another 25 years to live. So you need growth to cover inflation. Stock funds have historically returned about 7 percent over the inflation rate over the long term."

Growth-and-income funds. These funds invest in well-seasoned, blue-chip companies that have a track record of paying dividends. Some funds call themselves equity income funds, but there's not much difference between the two groups. Both have high dividend yields and focus on total return.

This type of fund is less risky than the growth-oriented funds because it invests in larger capitalized companies that have the cash flow to pay shareholders bigger dividends. And those dividends serve to cushion the blow from stock market declines.

Over the past 15 years, these funds, on average, have grown at an annual rate of 14 percent. But the funds are about 25 percent less volatile than those stocks indexed on the S&P 500.

Take Evergreen Total Return Fund, for instance, which yields around 7 percent. The fund has grown at an annual rate of 14 percent over the past decade. The fund, however, is almost 40 percent less volatile than the S&P 500 because it traditionally invested in higher yielding stocks and takes a small position in bonds.

Balanced funds. These all-weather funds focus on preservation of principal. A balanced fund will invest in a mixed portfolio of common stock, preferred stock, and bonds. Most balanced funds maintain a stock-to-bond ratio of 60:40. Balanced funds are less volatile than the stocks included in the S&P 500 or the Dow Jones Industrial Average. Investors receive income from high-yielding equities and fixed-income securities. Balanced funds will generally underperform in a bull market in stocks but will outperform the market during a recession.

Total return funds, which are a hybrid form of a balanced fund, give investors the opportunity for more profit potential. Total return portfolio managers have greater flexibility than have balanced fund managers. They can use market timing to move between stocks and fixed-income securities in any percentage they choose when investment conditions change. For example, in 1981, during a period of tight money, the Strong Total Return Fund rode up the yield curve by investing almost 100 percent in commercial paper when interest rates were rising. As interest rates fell, the fund picked up capital gains in bonds and moved into equities. Currently, the fund is almost 50 percent in cash, 33 percent in bonds, and the rest in stocks.

According to Jonathan Pond, president of Financial Planning Information, Inc., investors can get both a stock and bond position in a balanced fund; therefore these funds can serve as a core holding for safety-conscious investors. Because the funds maintain a stock-to-bond ratio of 60:40, you get part of your asset allocation done for you. So safety-conscious investors can round out their portfolios with growth funds, overseas funds, or income funds, depending on their level of risk.

Income funds. These funds seek a high level of current income for shareholders by investing in high-dividend-paying common stock and government and corporate bonds. The funds can be considered a more growth-oriented substitute for balanced funds.

Because a large part of their return is derived from interest and dividend income, however, the funds are more sensitive than other stock funds to changes in interest rates. So if interest rates rise, the fund's portfolio value will decline.

These funds also hold solid long-term growth stocks such as Texaco, NYNEX, AT&T, and Johnson & Johnson. According to Lipper Analytical Services, income funds may invest up to 60 percent in equities and up to 75 percent in bonds. This means that at any given time an income fund may have a 60 percent stock position and 40 percent bond position. On the other side, however, the most it can have in bonds is 75 percent. The fund would have to have 25 percent in equities.

Income funds currently yield between 5 percent and 9 percent. The Income Fund of America, for example, is yielding 8.6 percent and is about 40 percent invested in stocks. The fund, however, looks for capital growth and grew at an annual rate of 13 percent over the 15 years that ended in 1990.

Bond funds. Bond funds have several investment objectives. Some invest in long-term bonds, others in intermediate- and short-term notes. There are bond funds that invest only in the most creditworthy issuers—those companies whose debt obligations are rated A to triple-A (AAA) by Standard & Poor's and Moody's Investors Services. Lower-rated issuers pay higher yields because there is greater risk of default during economic recessions. Bonds rated double-B (BB) or lower are called junk bonds. Currently, mutual funds that invest in junk bonds are yielding 12 percent to 13 percent, or 4 percent more than Treasury securities, because investors are being compensated for greater risks.

There are also bond funds that invest in government securities. Funds that invest solely in U.S. Treasury securities carry no credit or default risk because the bonds are backed by the "full faith and credit" of Uncle Sam. Government securities funds also invest in U.S. government agency debt obligations. These funds invest primarily in Federal Home Loan Bank Board bonds and Government National Mortgage Association (GNMA, or "Ginnie Mae"), Federal National Mortgage Association (FNMA, or "Fannie Mae"), and Federal Home Loan Mortgage Corporation (popularly called "Freddie Mac") securities.

Government securities bond funds usually pay about 0.5 percent more than Treasury bonds for several reasons. First, U.S. government agency debt carries an implied moral obligation, not a full-faith and credit obligation, that the federal government will back up any defaults. Second, many government agencies issue mortgage bonds. As a result, both principal and interest are paid off to investors during the lifetime of the bond.

Government mortgage bond funds reinvest the principal and may distribute the interest to investors. In times of falling interest rates, however, homeowners tend to refinance their mortgages to take advantage of the lower rates. Thus investors may get both interest and principal back sooner than expected. Because the money would have to be reinvested at a rate not comparable with the original bond issue, the marketplace demands higher yields on these bonds. Currently, for example, Ginnie Mae bonds are yielding about 9.5 percent compared with 8.3 percent on long-term Treasury bonds.

Bond funds are not without risk. Although there is a low correlation between bond and equity returns, bond funds can be just as volatile as stocks. Bond prices move in opposite directions to interest rates. When interest rates rise, bond prices fall. In addition, the longer the maturity of the bond, the greater the price volatility.

Financial advisers stress that bond funds can act as a safety hedge against losses in stock funds. As a result, Don Phillips, publisher of *Mutual Fund Values*, Chicago, advises that younger investors keep about 25 percent of investment in bond funds. The closer you get to retirement, however, the more of your investment you should keep in bonds. Investors in their middle years, for example, should keep about 35 percent in bonds. Jonathan Pond believes senior citizens should have at least half of their money in bond funds of different maturities.

Money market funds. Money funds invest in short-term money market instruments. They invest in Treasury bills (T-bills), certificates of deposit (CDs), commercial paper, and repurchase agreements that are more than 100 percent collateralized. Because the funds are required to carry an average maturity of less than 125 days, they can maintain an unchanging net asset value (NAV) of $1. The net asset value is the price per share less expenses to operate the fund. There is no price volatility with money funds, but you earn lower yields.

Money funds also have check-writing privileges and can be used by corporate treasurers to concentrate daily cash balances or to pay bills. The safest money funds invest in Treasury bills and notes and other U.S. government agency obligations. The funds that pay the highest yields invest in money center bank CDs and commercial paper—IOUs of top-credit-rated corporations.

Overseas mutual funds. These funds come in two forms. Global funds can invest in both the U.S. and overseas stock markets. International funds exclude U.S. stocks and bonds from their portfolios. These funds are attractive because they offer an extra layer of diversification to mutual fund holdings. Many of the world's stock markets lead or lag the U.S. market. As a result, losses in U.S. holdings may be offset by gains overseas.

You can also invest in overseas bond funds. Foreign mutual funds, however, carry additional risks. Changes in the value of the dollar in relation to other currencies can affect the market value of overseas holdings. Investors also face political risks and must contend with the volatility of the indigenous markets.

Sector funds. Sector funds are specialized mutual funds. They invest in a specific industrial sector, such as health care, banking, technology, precious metals, chemicals, and drugs.

Fidelity Investments, Vanguard, and Financial Programs are three mutual fund groups that have a stable of sector funds. Fidelity Investments has the largest group of industry funds. Investors have 35 sectors to pick from. In addition, they have the option of being able to sell the mutual funds on the short side through Fidelity's discount brokerage operation.

Sector funds are a high-risk gambit because there is no diversification. If a specific industry is doing well, investors can make big profits. On the downside, however, investors can lose their shirts. For example, a few years ago, Fidelity Technology racked up double-digit gains and money flowed into the fund at an unprecedented rate. Then the bottom dropped out of the technology sector and the fund promptly dropped 50 percent in value. As a result, the experts advise that only sophisticated investors invest in sector funds.

Precious metals mutual funds, however, are often considered a long-term inflation hedge. Some financial planners recommend that investors keep 5 percent of their assets in precious metals. When inflation rises, bonds and stocks get hit hard, but gold and gold-related assets appreciate and balance out an investor's wealth.

Other types of sector funds can be used judiciously. For example, during bear markets and economic recessions, sectors in which the businesses are characterized by a stable demand for goods are considered safe harbors. Traditionally, utilities, defense, food, soaps, tobacco, and beverages are defensive investment sectors.

Whether you are 25 years old or 75 years old, mutual funds are one of the best ways for the average person to save for the long term. As Figure 1.1 demonstrates, investing in mutual funds is one of the few ways in which the average wage earner can build substantial wealth. Granted, past performance is not necessarily an indication of future results. However, if you had invested $10,000 in the Investment Company of America Fund 50 years ago, your investment would be worth almost $4 million today. That's equivalent to making about 12.2 percent annually on your investment. Your money doubled every six years.

And if you invest right—that is, diversify your investment among stocks, bonds, and cash—you can buy or hold and get a good night's sleep for years to come. Studies by the *L/G No Load Fund Analyst*, a San Francisco–based mutual fund newsletter, show, for example, that if you had divided your portfolio into two-thirds stocks and one-third bonds, your investment would have grown at an annual rate of 9.8 percent over 54 years. Not bad.

CHAPTER 2

How Mutual Funds Work

Investment company: another name for a mutual fund company

prospectus: the legal document that investors are required to read before they invest to learn important information about investment objectives, risks, fees, and the fund's management

adviser: an investment professional hired to provide investment advice and management to a mutual fund company

When you invest in a mutual fund, you become a shareholder of a portfolio of securities. You are a part owner, along with others, who have hired an *investment company* to manage money based on the shareowners' investment objectives.

As an owner, you elect a board of directors that is responsible for seeing to it that your money is invested based on the objectives of the fund. These objectives are stated in the fund *prospectus*, which you are required to read before investing in a fund. Upon request, a "statement of additional information" will be sent to prospective investors. This document provides investors with more detailed information about the fund, its risks, and its investment objective.

The board of directors has a lot of work to do on your behalf. It appoints officers to take care of the daily business. The directors also hire a management company to invest your hard-earned cash.

The management company is the organization that makes a fund available to the investing public. The management company hires an investment *adviser* to run the fund. In addition, the management company charges you a fee for its services. Management fees usually range from between 0.5 percent and 1 percent of the total assets under management.

Most funds also do business with a custodian, transfer agent, and underwriter. The custodian is usually a bank. The *custodian bank* is in charge of safeguarding the fund's assets, making payments for the fund's portfolio of securities, and receiving payments when securities are sold.

custodian bank: a bank responsible for custody of fund shares, which are kept in a separate account from other assets

The *transfer agent* performs the record keeping for the shareholders. The transfer agent is responsible for issuing new shares, canceling and redeeming shares, and distributing dividends and capital gains to shareholders.

transfer agent: a company hired by the mutual fund to keep shareholder account records

The principal underwriter of the mutual fund distributes the fund shares to the publc. An underwriter sells fund shares to a securities dealer or directly to the public. Underwriters are middlepeople who distribute the funds to stock *broker dealers*, financial planners, insurance agents, bankers, or the investment public.

broker dealers: companies that buy and sell fund shares to investors (Underwriters sell funds to broker dealers who in turn sell fund shares to investors.)

HOW FUNDS ARE SOLD

Fund shares are distributed to the public in a variety of ways:

• No-load mutual funds, or funds free of sales charges, are sold directly to the public. Investors learn about no-load funds from advertising, direct mail marketing, or from mutual fund newsletters.

• Low-load and some no-load funds may charge shareholders a distribution fee, known as a 12b-1 fee. The revenues from this fee are used to market the fund so that the public is aware of the investment.

• Load funds are marketed through a sales force such as stockbrokers, financial planners, and insurance agents. These financial advisers may be compensated for their services to the investors through a direct sales commission included in the price of the fund shares, through a 12b-1 distribution fee paid by the fund, or both ways.

UNDERSTANDING THE MUTUAL FUND PROSPECTUS

The prospectus is a legal document that provides you with all the important information you need to know about the fund before you invest. The prospectus covers 17 areas about your investment. You should be sure to read the document carefully before you invest. By law, the investment company cannot sell you fund shares until you have read the prospectus. You should also keep the prospectus on file, so you can refer to it if you have any questions about your investment in the future.

Here are the basic components of the mutual fund prospectus based on the Investment Company Institute's publication called *An Investor's Guide to Reading the Mutual Fund Prospectus*. (You can obtain a free copy of this publication by writing the Investment Company Institute, 1600 M Street NW, Suite 600, Washington, DC 20036.)

1. *Name of the fund and the date of the prospectus.* The prospectus is usually updated every year to reflect any changes in the fund.

2. *Required cover statement.* This is a statement that says you should read the prospectus before you invest. This section also tells you where to call to get an extra statement of information about the fund. The statement of information lists in more detail how the fund is managed and the risks involved.

3. *Required disclaimer.* This statement is required by the Securities and Exchange Commission. The disclaimer says it is up to you to accept or reject the investment decisions of the fund. That means that you have the power to buy or sell your shares in the fund. If the fund performs poorly, you are responsible for your losses because you chose to invest in the fund.

4. *Statement of investment objectives.* This tells you the *investment objectives* of the fund. It may be long-term growth; it could be income and preservation of principal. The investment objective depends on the type of fund you buy.

5. *Fee table.* This is a table that lists the front-end or deferred sales charges that you must pay. It lists the *management fees*, 12b-1 fees, and other expenses. The operating expenses are also listed. Table 2.1 is a hypothetical example of the expenses you would pay on a $1,000 investment.

6. *Per-share table.* This table appears along with the fee table at the beginning of the prospectus. It lists important per-share information about the fund for the past year. You see in dollars per share the following information:

- Investment income
- Expenses
- Net investment income or income less expenses
- Dividends from net investment income
- Distributions from net realized capital gains (That's the profit on the sale of securities less expenses.)
- Net increase or decrease in the *net asset value* of the fund
- Net asset value at the beginning of the year
- Net asset value at the end of the year
- Ratio of expenses to average net assets
- Ratio of net investment income to average net assets
- Portfolio turnover rate
- Number of shares outstanding

Table 2.2 shows an example of a per-share table.

7. *Performance.* The prospectus gives you information about the yield and total return of the

Investment objectives: a description of a fund's investment plan (Stock funds that invest for growth look for capital appreciation. Some funds invest for both growth and income. Other funds preserve capital by investing in both stocks and bonds. Fixed-income funds invest for safety, liquidity, or yield.)

management fees: fees a fund pays to its investment adviser

net asset value (NAV): price of the fund per share net of fund expenses (Funds with sales loads have two share prices—the offering price, which reflects NAV plus sales charges, and the redemption price, which is the NAV the broker charges to buy back the shares.)

Table 2.1. Mutual Fund Fees

Shareholder Transaction Expenses	Fund ABC	Fund XYZ
Maximum sales load imposed on purchases (as a percentage of offering price)	5.75%	0
Maximum sales load imposed on reinvested dividends	0	0
Contingent deferred sales charge	0	5%*
Redemption fee	0	0
Exchange fee	0	$ 5†
Wire transfer of redemption proceeds	0	$10
Annual Operating Expenses (as a percentage of average net assets)		
Management fees	0.5%	0.6%
12b-1 fees	0	0.25%
Other expenses	0.4%	0.2%
Total operating expenses:	0.9%	1.05%

Source: Investment Company Institute, Washington, DC.

*There is a 5% sales charge imposed on redemptions made within the first year after purchase; a 4% charge on redemptions made during the second year; 3% during the third year; 2% during the fourth; and 1% during the fifth year following purchase. There is no sales charge for redemptions made in the sixth year after purchase or in subsequent years.

†There is no fee on the first four exchanges each year.

fund. Total return measures the gain or loss in the net asset value of the fund with reinvestment of dividends and/or capital gains. You can compare the performance of your potential investment with other funds and the market averages.

Table 2.2.   Per-Share Table

Per-Share Income and Capital Changes
Year Ended x/x/19xx

Investment income	$.21	The pro rata (per-share) income the fund earned on its investments.
Expenses	.05	The pro rata expenses the fund incurred (costs of doing business).
Net investment income	.16	Income less expenses; nearly all of this income must be distributed to shareholders.
Dividends from net investment income	(.14)	Per-share distributions from net investment income; your dividends per share.
Net realized and unrealized gain (loss) on investments	.70	The fund's capital gains and losses on the sale of its investments (realized) and appreciation or depreciation of the value of its investments (unrealized); nearly all of the net realized gains must be distributed to shareholders.
Distributions from net realized gain	(.63)	The pro rata share of capital gains distributions to shareholders.
Net increase (decrease) in net asset value	.09	The amount of undistributed capital gains or losses and appreciation or depreciation (here a gain of 7¢), if any, plus undistributed net investment income (here 2¢), if any.
Net asset value: beginning of year	5.65	The beginning per-share value of the fund's portfolio of investments and other assets, less any liabilities and accrued expenses.
Net asset value: end of year	5.74	The ending per-share value of the fund's portfolio of investments and other assets, less any liabilities and accrued expenses; includes any undistributed income or gains for the year plus the change in appreciation or depreciation of the fund's investments since the beginning of the year.

(Continued)

Table 2.2. *(Continued)*

Per-Share Income and Capital Changes
                    Year Ended x/x/19xx

Ratio of expenses to average net assets	0.88%	The total of all the fund's operating expenses divided by the average net assets under management for that year.
Ratio of net investment income to average net assets	2.81%	The fund's total net investment income divided by the average net assets under management for that year.
		For this hypothetical fund, these two ratios indicate that, for every $10,000 in net assets, after paying $88 in expenses, the fund had $281 in income remaining.
Portfolio turnover rate	61%	A measure of the trading activity in the fund's portfolio of investments.
Number of shares outstanding (in thousands) at end of year	39,504	This fund has about 39.5 million shares outstanding; to calculate its total assets ($226,752,960), multiply the number of shares times the end-of-year net asset value per share.

Source: Investment Company Institute, Washington, DC.

8. *Investment policies.* This section tells you the investment objectives of the fund. It tells about the methods used to select securities.

9. *Investment risks.* This section spells out the risks of the investments. It also explains the investment restrictions of the fund.

10. *Portfolio turnover.* This section tells you how often the fund manager trades securities. A fund with 100 percent portfolio turnover means the entire composition of the fund's portfolio changes in a year's time.

11. *Information about the fund's investment adviser.* This section lists the name and address of the firm that manages the fund's investments. It also gives information about the experience of the investment adviser firm, services offered, and fees.

12. *Information about the transfer agent.* This part lists the name and address of the transfer agent of the fund. The transfer agent keeps the shareholder records and prepares statements.

13. *Shareholder rights.* This section tells you that you will receive the same return for each dollar you invest that every other shareholder in the fund receives.

14. *Distributions.* This section tells you when your dividends and capital gains are declared and when they are paid.

15. *Taxes on earnings.* You will pay an income tax on the earnings of your fund unless you invest in municipal bond funds, which are tax free.

16. *How to buy shares.* This section tells you how to purchase shares and where to send the money. It lists minimum initial and subsequent investments for retirement and nonretirement accounts. You will also read about automatic investments.

17. *How to redeem shares.* This section tells you how to sell shares, whom to talk to, and the procedure for redemption.

OTHER IMPORTANT FUND DOCUMENTS

Once you invest, you will receive other important reports from the fund. Every three months you will receive a quarterly investment report. The fund manager or president of the fund usually writes a section describing the performance of the fund and the outlook for the fund. The report also lists the performance of the fund over the recent period, for one year, and for the life of the fund. It lists a breakdown of the portfolio holdings in the fund.

The annual report gives you a rundown on how the fund did for the entire year. The president of the fund will also talk about the outlook for the financial market in the future. You will also get a list of the portfolio holdings in the fund.

At the time of this writing, the Securities and Exchange Commission came out with new mutual fund prospectus rules. Fund prospectuses and annual reports are now required to disclose the following information:

- The name and title of the portfolio manager. Funds managed by a committee and index funds are not bound by this rule.
- A discussion of the fund's performance. Annual reports and prospectuses will explain what happened during the past year and why.
- Each fund must now provide a graph showing the fund's performance in comparison to relevant indexes over the previous ten years. Graphs must show what a hypothetical $10,000 investment grew to and reflect all fund expenses, sales loads, and account fees.

THE RIGHT WAY TO REGISTER YOUR MUTUAL FUNDS

There's a right way and a wrong way to fill out your mutual fund application when you invest but, according to Rudy Watz, a New York–based financial planner who has worked in the mutual fund industry for more than a decade, there is no best way to register your mutual fund accounts. "It depends on each individual's set of circumstances and their tax bracket," he says. In his proprietary newsletter, Watz offers the following advice to his clients on how to register their mutual fund investments.

There are three ways to own property—whether it's a mutual fund or a piece of real estate:

- *Fee simple.* This means you own all of it.
- *Tenancy in common.* If you own something as tenancy in common, you own part of it and can

give, sell, or leave your part of the property to others when you die.

• *Joint tenancy.* You own all the property with someone else. You can give your interest away or sell it, but you can't leave your interest to someone else when you die.

Here are how some of the options work when you fill out your mutual fund's application form.

Type of registration. Bob, an unmarried investor, checks the "joint registration" box on the mutual fund application and lists his daughter Nancy as the joint registrant. When Bob dies, Nancy becomes the sole owner of all shares in the account, even if Bob's will says that all of his estate is to go to his other daughter, Sally.

Bob could have avoided cutting out Sally, Watz says, by doing the following: If Bob had indicated on the application that he wanted "tenancy in common," with Nancy listed as the tenant in common, upon Bob's death, only half of the shares would go to Nancy. The other half would go to Sally.

Income and estate tax implications. Watz says that the title of the account registration can also affect how much income and estate taxes may have to be paid by an investor's heirs.

For example, assume Tom invested $20,000 in a mutual fund and named his son Ted as the joint registrant on the application. At the time of Tom's death, the mutual fund shares had increased in value to $50,000. If Ted is the "joint registrant" with "right of survivorship," the entire $50,000 will be included in Tom's gross estate for estate tax purposes and Ted becomes the sole owner of the account.

What about the $30,000 in appreciation in the

value of the mutual fund? Will Ted be subject to income taxes when he sells the shares right after Tom's death (assuming no further appreciation)? Watz says the answer is no because the tax basis of all Tom's shares is stepped up to fair market value at the time of Tom's death.

In contrast, if Ted was registered instead as "joint registrant" with "tenancy in common," and Tom is deemed to have made a gift of half of the original investment to Ted, only half of the $50,000 would be included in Tom's gross estate. Ted now owns only half the account—$25,000. In addition, $15,000 will be subject to income taxes when Ted sells.

If you have a sizable estate or are concerned about how your heirs will receive your money, consult with your financial planner or accountant before you invest.

"Think carefully about how you register your mutual fund accounts," stresses Watz. "The choice can affect who will inherit the money after your death and how much tax your heirs will have to pay. In all but the simplest situations, it may be prudent to consult with your financial adviser on how to best register your accounts."

HOW TO READ NEWSPAPER MUTUAL FUND TABLES

Well, you've read over several prospectuses and you've got a notion to invest some of your hard-earned cash in a fund. Now you want to check the net asset value or price of the fund at the close of yesterday's business day. The illustration in Figure 2.1, designed by the Investment Company Institute, explains how to read the mutual fund table in the newspaper.

When you look at the mutual fund table in the

The first column is the abbreviated fund's name. Several funds listed under a single heading indicate a family of funds.

The second column is the Net Asset Value (NAV) per share as of the close of the preceding business day. In some newspapers, the NAV is identified as the sell or the bid price—the amount (per share) you would receive if you sold your shares amount (per share) you would receive if you sold your shares (less any deferred sales charges). Each mutual fund determines its net asset value every business day by dividing the market value of its total assets, less liabilities, by the number of shares outstanding. On any given day, you can determine the value of your holdings by multiplying the NAV by the number of shares you own.

The third column is the offering price or, in some papers, the buy or the asked price— the price you would pay is you purchased shares. The buy price is the NAV plus any sales charges. If there are no sales charges, and NL for no-load appears in this column, the buy price is the same as the NAV. To figure the sales charge percentage, divide the difference between the NAV and the offering price by the offering price. Here, for instance, the sales charge is 7.2 percent ($14.52 − 13.47 = $1.05; $1.05 ÷ $14.52 = 0.072).

The fourth column shows the change, if any, in net asset value from the preceding quotation—in other words, the change over the most recent one-day trading period. This fund, for example, gained eight cents per share.

Source: Investment Company Institute, Washington, DC. Used with permission.

Figure 2.1. How to read the mutual fund table in the newspaper.

newspaper, you will also see small letters beside a fund's name. These letters are references to footnotes giving important information. Here is what the letters mean:

- An *e* stands for ex-distribution, meaning the fund is paying out dividend and/or capital gains distributions.
- An *x* stands for ex-dividend, also known as the ex-dividend date of the fund. (The date a mutual fund goes ex-dividend is the time between the announcement and payment of dividends. Anyone buying shares during this time will not collect dividends.)
- An *f* stands for the previous day's quotation.
- *NL* stands for no load.
- A *p* stands for a 12b-1 fee.
- An *r* stands for a redemption charge.
- A *t* stands for both a 12b-1 and a redemption charge.

HOW TO CALCULATE THE RETURN ON YOUR INVESTMENT

Once you buy your mutual fund or funds, how do you tell how well the fund is performing?

Both bond and stock funds distribute dividends and capital gains. Dividends come from interest payments received on bonds. Dividend income also comes in the form of a company's earnings, which it distributes to its shareholders. In the case of mutual funds, the fund collects the dividends for you.

Capital gain income comes from the sale of securities at a profit. You can also have capital losses. A mutual fund can carry forward its losses, but any gains, less loss carried forward, are distributed to shareholders at least once a year.

Most mutual funds reinvest dividend and/or capital gains distributions on the ex-dividend date. This is the date the shareholders of record receive their distributions. If you invest after a fund goes ex-dividend, you will not collect any income. In most cases, a mutual fund's net asset value will increase by the dollar amount of the dividend as the ex-dividend date approaches. But then the net asset value falls by the amount of the distribution after the ex-dividend date.

A few mutual funds will reinvest your distributions on the record date or pay date. The record date is the date by which a mutual fund shareholder must own shares in order to receive dividend and/ or capital gains distribution. The pay date is the actual date on which the distributions are paid to the shareholders. Total return is a calculation that includes the price appreciation in the fund's net asset value or share price, plus the reinvestment of dividends and capital gains.

How to Figure Your Total Return

First, write down the number of shares purchased and multiply that number by the net asset value (NAV) at the time you invested to get the dollar value of your investment.

Second, take the dollar amount of any dividends and/or capital gains distributions and divide that number into the net asset value on the date when the distributions would be reinvested. This gives you the number of shares you reinvest into more fund shares.

Third, total up the number of shares you now own and multiply that by the current net asset value listed in today's newspaper. This gives you the market value of your investment.

Fourth, compute the percentage change—plus

Table 2.3. Worksheet for Calculating Total Return

Initial purchase $:

Initial NAV:

Initial number of shares:

Distribution $:

Reinvestment NAV:

New shares: Distribution $/reinvested NAV =

Total shares owned: Initial shares + reinvested shares =

Market value of investment: Current NAV × total shares = $

Total return: Initial investment − market value/initial
investment = %

or minus—in your initial investment compared
with the market value of your investment with dividends and capital gains reinvested. You do this
by subtracting your market value from your initial
investment and dividing that number by the value
of your initial investment. This gives you the percent change in your investment.

For example, say you bought 1,000 shares of
the Flying Wallenda's Growth Stock fund at a net
asset value of $10. Your initial investment is
$10,000. Three months later the fund declared a
distribution of 10 cents per share. That means you
got 10 cents times 1,000 shares or $100 of dividends
from the fund. The net asset value of the fund at
the time the dividends were reinvested was $10.10.
So $100 divided by $10.10 means you own 9.9 additional shares. The total amount of shares you now
own is 1009.9.

A little later in the year you want to figure the
total return on your investment. The NAV of the
fund now stands at $10.50. So $10.50 times 1009.9
shares equals $10,603.95.

The value of your investment grew by $603.95,

or to $10,603.95 from $10,000. This represents a return of 6.04 percent, or $603.95 divided by $10,000.

Use the worksheet shown in Table 2.3 to calculate the returns on your investments.

CHAPTER 3

The Investment Risks

There's no free lunch when it comes to investing in stocks, bonds, or even bank certificates of deposit (CDs), which are federally insured. Before you invest in mutual funds, you have to understand the *risk*. Once you know how a particular type of mutual fund will perform during good and bad times, you can pick the fund that's right for you.

risk: factors such as inflation, rising interest rates, defaults by bond issuers, poor financial performance by a company, or downward movements in the financial markets that may cause stock or bond prices to drop

FACING AND FINESSING THE RISKS

Here is a review of the risks you'll likely run up against when you buy a stock or fixed-income mutual fund. Also included are ways to reduce the risks of losing money.

Market timing. You could find yourself investing in bonds or stocks at a market peak, only to find the markets declining after you've paid out your money. What happens if you put a big sum of money into a stock fund and then the stock market tumbles? No doubt you will be upset. Dollar cost averaging is one surefire way to reduce market-timing risk.

With dollar cost averaging, you invest a certain amount every month. That way you continue to buy shares when prices drop. Over the long term, the average cost of your investment will be much less than the market price when you decide to cash out.

Lost opportunity. Many investors like the safety of federally insured certificates of deposit (CDs). But buying CDs involves risk, too—you could find yourself locked into a CD as interest rates are rising.

If you stagger your CD maturities from one to five years, for example, you can avoid the lost opportunity risk. The same goes for bond funds. You may earn a high average yield, but you also have money that's maturing early. In the case of CDs, if you put one-fifth in CDs with maturities ranging from one to five years, 20 percent of your money will be maturing every year. That way, you may find yourself investing at higher rates.

Credit risk. You could be attracted to the high yields offered by junk bonds with low credit ratings. In a recession, however, issuers with lower credit-rated companies may have a hard time paying back principal and interest to lenders. One way to reduce credit risk is to stick with U.S. government Treasury bonds, notes, and bills. These bonds carry the full faith and credit obligation of Uncle Sam. There is no risk of default. U.S. government agency obligations are also considered to have no credit risk. These issues are backed by the implied moral obligation of the government against default.

Corporate bonds that carry single-A (A) to triple-A (AAA) credit ratings by Standard & Poor's and Moody's Investors Services are also considered high-grade investments. Triple-A-rated firms are considered the most creditworthy issuers on the market.

Interest-rate risk. Bond prices and interest rates move in opposite directions. If interest rates rise, bond prices decline. The longer the maturity on the bond, the greater the price drop. For example, if interest rates rose 1 percent, your 20-year 9 percent bond would lose about 10 percent of its market value. A short-term note with a maturity of 10 years would lose about half that much.

The rule of thumb: The shorter the maturity, the less the price volatility. When interest rates rise, bond funds that own securities maturing in two to five years are half as volatile as long-term bond funds.

Diversification risk. If you don't plan your investments carefully, you could find yourself holding a limited number or type of stocks or bonds that are unhedged. You might make big profits, but you'd have nothing to balance out potential losses.

To protect yourself from a few issues in a few industries doing poorly, you have to do the following:

1. Own a broadly diversified mutual fund that holds a large number of issues across different industries.

2. Diversify among different types of mutual funds to help cut your losses. For example, look what happened on April 7, 1992. The stock market dropped a hair under 2 percent in one day. But bond prices went up and Treasury bills (T-bills) yielded 4 percent. So if you had kept one-third of your investments in stocks, bonds, and T-bills or money funds, you would have lost only one-third of 1 percent.

In other words, if you had 100 percent of your money or, say, $10,000 in a stock fund, you would have been down $200 that day. With a one-third stock, bond, and money fund split, your investment would have dropped only $33 in value.

Purchasing power risk. Inflation will eat away at how much your money can buy in years to come. If the cost of goods and services goes up and you own a bond that pays a fixed rate of interest, you are in trouble. You've lost purchasing power.

Say, for example, you get $1,000 a year interest from a bond. You get that amount every year. That grand will buy you so many items. But the cost of the items goes up every year so, over time, you will be able to buy less and less with your interest income.

If inflation grows at 5 percent a year, groceries that cost $1 today will cost $2 in 14 years. That doesn't bode well for the $1,000 in principal you will get back when your bond matures in 14 years.

In other words, the $1,000 can buy only $500 worth of goods 14 years from now. There are ways to reduce purchasing power risks, however. Put part of your portfolio in stocks. According to Ibbotson Associates data, stocks historically earned 6.5 percent to 7 percent annually above the inflation rate. Also consider investing in precious metals and funds that invest in the energy industry. During periods of high inflation, these investments tend to perform well.

More Risks

You face a couple of other risks when you invest in individual securities or a portfolio of securities like a mutual fund.

Systematic risk. If the entire stock market declines, your stock or stock fund will fall right along with it. In the halls of finance, this is known as systematic or market risk. Financial research has shown that about 60 percent of the time a stock's price moves with the market. About 10 percent of the time luck plays a factor in whether a stock goes up or down in price. About 20 percent of the time, specific information about a company, its industry, or the economy may affect the stock's price. For example, say a stock market analyst's report on XYZ company is highly favorable because of the company's marketing program and cost-cutting measures of the past year. The stock's price zooms up $3 a share. Or, say EFG's chief financial officer dies unexpectedly in a car accident. EFG's stock price may drop $2.25 a share in response to the bad news.

Unsystematic risk. Specific news about a company or industry is called unsystematic risk by the academics. If you own one or two stocks in a single industry, such news can push the stocks up or down. The way to protect yourself against the impact of bad news on a company's stock price is to diversify and own a large number of stocks in a large number of industries. Then, if a few stocks in your portfolio do poorly, the loss won't hurt the performance of your entire holdings.

HOW FAR SHOULD YOU STICK YOUR NECK OUT?

The greater the potential payoff, the greater the risk. Investors are compensated for sticking their necks out. But how far is too far?

Over the long term, a risky asset may have a great yield record; but when times get tough, investors have to sell because they need money. That drives prices down. If you can't hold on for the rebound, you are vulnerable. But if you're not wiped out over the recessionary short term by that

16-percent high-yielding junk bond, you will collect a lot of interest income.

The same goes for aggressive stock and small-company stock funds. In 1991, these funds gained 47.73 percent and 51.53 percent, respectively. You can lose, too. Aggressive stock funds lost 8.6 percent and small-company stock funds lost 9.72 percent in 1990.

Over the long term, what can you expect to earn or lose when you invest in stocks and bonds? Over the past six decades, statistics published by Ibbotson & Associates show the following:[1]

• Stocks have grown at an average annual rate of 10 percent a year. But the price swing—called the standard deviation in the performance—is 21 percent. That means you face about a two-thirds chance of making between 11 and 31 percent in any given year.

• U.S. government bonds grew at an annual rate of 4.3 percent. The price swing is 8.5 percent. So you have about a two-thirds chance of making between 12.8 percent and 4.2 percent in any given year.

• T-bills grew at an annual rate of 3.4 percent. But you have about a two-thirds chance of making between 6.8 percent and 0 percent in any given year.

• Small-company stocks grew at an annual rate of 12.1 percent. But you have about a two-thirds chance of making between 38 percent and 23.8 percent in any given year.

• Foreign stocks grew at an annual rate of 13.2 percent. But you have about a two-thirds chance of making between 33.3 percent and 7.1 percent in any given year.

[1] *Stocks, Bonds Bills, and Inflation 1993 Yearbook*™, Ibbotson Associates, Chicago (annual update of work by Roger G. Ibbotson and Rex A. Sinquefield). All rights reserved. Used with permission.

• Foreign bonds grew at an annual rate of 8.7 percent. But you have a two-thirds chance of making between 18.8 percent or 2.6 percent in any given year.

• Inflation grew at an annual rate of 3 percent. But two-thirds of the time it can range between 7.8 percent or drop to 1.8 percent in any given year.

Financial assets can be very risky over the short term, but they can pay off handsomely if you buy and hold for the longer term.

Steve Norwitz, spokesperson for T. Rowe Price Group of Mutual Funds, notes that over 1-year investment periods, common stocks are extremely volatile, with returns ranging from 52.6 percent in 1954 to −26.5 percent in 1974.

Consider the following statistics:

• Over 5-year holding periods, the range between the best and worst returns is 25 percent and 5 percent, respectively.
• Over 10-year periods, the range is 20 percent and 3 percent, respectively.
• Over 20-year periods, the range is 12 percent and 8 percent, respectively.

The lesson to be learned from these numbers is that the longer you hold your stock funds, the greater your chance of making money. But if you try to get rich quick, you may or may not. The shorter the holding period, the greater the risk of losing money.

James Cloonan, president of the American Association of Individual Investors in Chicago, notes that if you hold stocks for 10 years or more, there's not much chance you will lose money. Over the past 60 years, if you had bought and held stocks in any 10-year period since 1926, you would have had a loss only 4 percent of the time. By contrast, if you bought at the beginning of the year and sold at the end of the year, you would have lost money 30 percent of the time in every 1-year period over the last six decades.

KNOW WHAT'S RISKY AND WHAT'S NOT

Before you invest in a mutual fund, it's important to understand the investment objectives of the fund. You want to find the best mix of investments that gives you the highest return with the least amount of risk. The investment pyramid (Figure 3.1) illustrates the most and least risky assets. Riskier investments have the greatest price volatility and expose you to the greatest losses. You should study this illustration before you start your diversified investment plan.

At the top of the pyramid are the "boom or bust" investments. These might earn you 100 percent on your investment, or they might evaporate in front of your eyes. At the next level are investments in which you can expect to earn an average of 15 percent to 25 percent in any given year, or lose as much as 20 percent.

In the upper-bottom half of the pyramid are mutual fund investments. These funds hold a large number of issues and are generally considered safer than individual securities. Precious metals and over-the-counter stock mutual funds, however, can be risky; blue-chip stocks are less risky; and balanced funds that keep half their assets in stocks and bonds are very conservative vehicles. At the bottom of the pryamid are the most secure choices, such as government securities, which are guaranteed against default. Buyers do, of course, face risk from fluctuating interest rates; this is also the case with other low-risk investments, including short-term T-bills, federally insured bank CDs, and money funds.

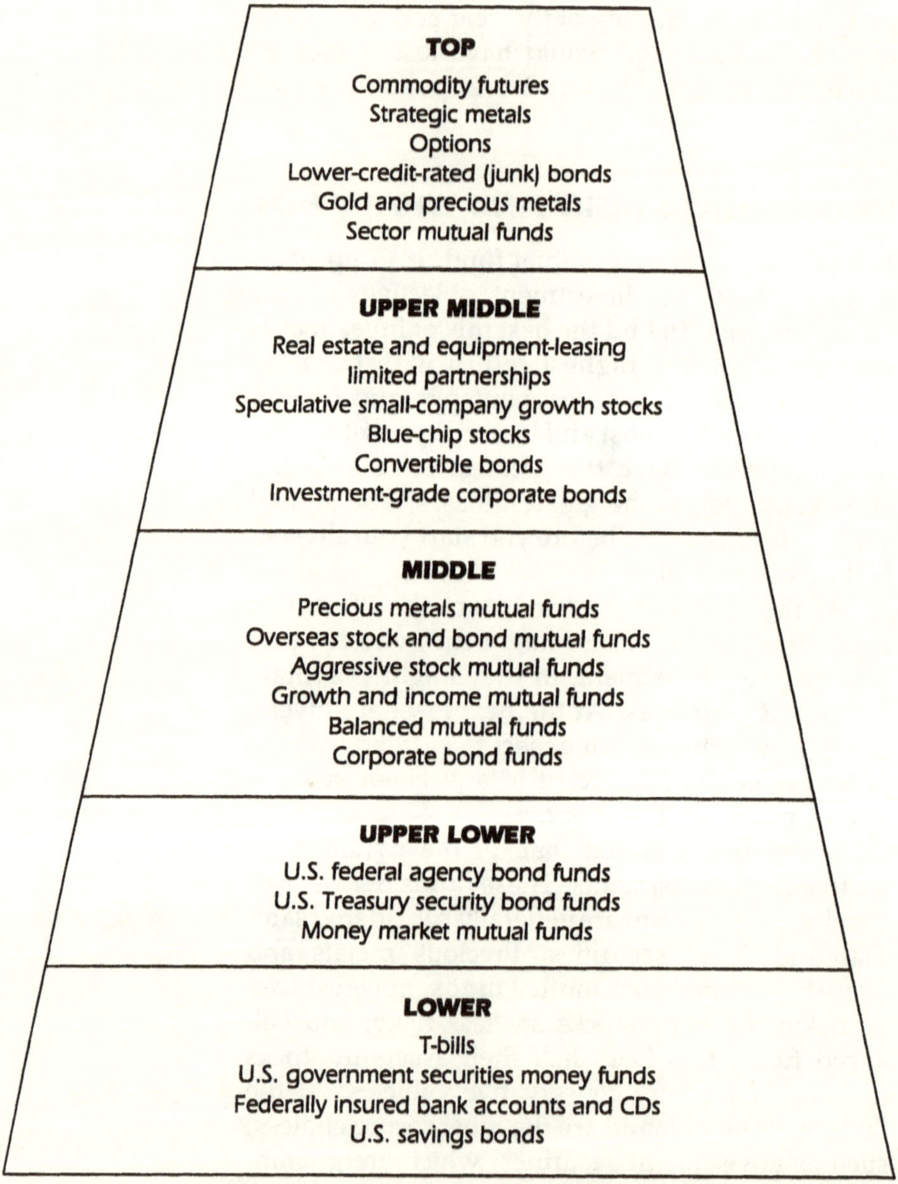

TOP

Commodity futures
Strategic metals
Options
Lower-credit-rated (junk) bonds
Gold and precious metals
Sector mutual funds

UPPER MIDDLE

Real estate and equipment-leasing
limited partnerships
Speculative small-company growth stocks
Blue-chip stocks
Convertible bonds
Investment-grade corporate bonds

MIDDLE

Precious metals mutual funds
Overseas stock and bond mutual funds
Aggressive stock mutual funds
Growth and income mutual funds
Balanced mutual funds
Corporate bond funds

UPPER LOWER

U.S. federal agency bond funds
U.S. Treasury security bond funds
Money market mutual funds

LOWER

T-bills
U.S. government securities money funds
Federally insured bank accounts and CDs
U.S. savings bonds

Figure 3.1.   Investment pyramid of risk.

CHAPTER 4

What Kind of Risk Taker Are You?

N ow that you have an idea from Chapter 3 about the different types of risks involved in mutual fund investing and how mutual funds differ, it's important to understand how much risk you are willing to take.

DETERMINING YOUR RISK LEVEL

Try answering the questions developed by Michael Lipper, president of Lipper Analytical Services in New York. Lipper's questionnaire is one of the best around because it puts a clear focus on the risk-return relationship.

Get out a pen and paper or scribble in the margins of this book and try out the risk test. If you score 5, you have a low tolerance for risk. A score of 10 means you're a moderate investor; while a score of 25 designates you as a risk taker. Circle your answers and add up the numbers.

• My investment is for the long term; the end result is more important than how I go about achieving it. (1) Totally disagree. (2) Can accept variability, but not loss of capital. (3) Can accept reasonable amounts of price fluctuation in total return. (4) Can accept an occasional year of negative performance in the interest of building capital. (5) Agree.

• Rank the importance of current income. (1) Essential and must be known. (2) Essential but willing to accept uncertainty about the amount. (3) Important, but there are other factors to consider. (4) Modest current income is desirable. (5) Irrelevant.

• Rank the amount of decline you can accept in a single quarter. (1) None. (2) A little, but not for the entire year. (3) Consistency of results is more important than outperforming the market. (4) A few quarters of decline is a small price to pay to be invested when the stock market takes off. (5) Unimportant. Capital and income are more important. (2,3,4) Willing to invest to beat inflation, but other investment needs come first. (5) Essential to ensure a real return on my investment.

• Rank the importance of beating the stock market over the economic cycle. (1) Irrelevant. (2,3,4) Prefer consistency over superior results. (5) Critical.

WHAT SHOULD YOU INVEST IN BASED ON YOUR RISK SCORE?

Add up your risk score and refer to Table 4.1 to learn when mutual fund investments are best for you.

If you scored 5 or less on the test, you want safety, liquidity, and yield. You should consider federally insured CDs, T-bills, or money market funds, and U.S. government or high-grade bond funds and utility stocks.

Those with scores between 5 and 10 are willing to assume modest risk in return for long-term growth. Invest a small percentage of your investment in growth funds, growth-and-income funds,

Table 4.1.   Determining Your Risk Level

Your Needs	Risk Level	Types of Investments
Safety, liquidity, and yield	Very low	T-bills, bank CDs, money funds, bank accounts.
Safety and yield	Low	Treasury notes, short-term bonds, government agency securities, fixed-income mutual funds.
Growth and/or income	Moderate	Dividend income funds, blue-chip high-yielding stocks or mutual funds, utility stocks, preferred stocks.
Growth	Higher	Gold, individual aggressive growth stocks and mutual funds, high-yielding stocks and bond funds, foreign securities.

Source: Morningstar Mutual Funds, Chicago. Used with permission.

income funds, balanced funds that own both stocks and bonds, and money funds.

If you scored between 10 and 25, you have the stomach to tolerate the short-term volatility in the stock market in return for longer-term gains. Those willing to assume more risk often prefer to invest in aggressive growth and small-company stock funds. Venturesome investors who are a little more conservative frequently invest in growth-and-income funds for total return.

HOW TO DIVIDE UP YOUR INVESTMENT PIE

No matter what kind of risk taker you are, the experts say you should not keep all of your eggs in one basket. Dr. Gerald Perritt, editor of the *Mutual*

Fund Letter and *Mutual Fund Encyclopedia* in Chicago, says you should diversify your investments as a hedge against losses. The more aggressive you are, the more money you keep in stocks. The more conservative you are, the more you keep in bonds and money funds.

Dr. Perritt suggests you adhere to the following mixes based on your tolerance for risk:

- Highly aggressive investors should keep 28 percent in money funds and 72 percent in aggressive growth, small-company stock, and growth stock mutual funds.
- Moderately aggressive investors should keep 33 percent in money funds and 67 percent in aggressive growth, small-company stock, and growth stock mutual funds.
- Conservative investors who want some growth should consider keeping 28 percent in money funds and 72 percent in growth-and-income funds.
- Safety-minded investors who want income and some growth should keep 35 percent in money funds and 65 percent in high-dividend-yielding stock funds or growth-and-income funds.

CHAPTER 5

How to Pick a Mutual Fund That Is Right for You

Believe it or not, there are more mutual funds on the market today than there are stocks traded on the New York stock exchanges.

Now that there are more than 4,000 mutual funds to pick from, it's not an easy task to find the fund that's right for you. You have to do some homework before you invest. If you invest in no-load funds, you will have to do your own legwork. You can go to the public library and look through the performance reports of the CDA/Wiesenberger Investment Company Service or Morningstar Mutual Funds for a list of the best-performing funds. Or you can subscribe to one of several excellent mutual fund newsletters that recommend funds.

If you have a stockbroker or financial planner to pick funds for you, you'll pay him or her a front- or back-end load and other fees for helping you put together a mutual fund investment portfolio.

Regardless of whether you do it yourself, rely on newsletter recommendations, or pay a broker, you should use the following criteria to select the best mutual funds that meet your financial needs, goals, and tolerance for risk.

In this chapter, you will read about how to compare mutual funds. You will read about how some of the leading mutual fund advisers pick funds. In addition, you will learn how to evaluate the performance of your fund.

HOW TO SELECT A FUND

Here are the important factors you have to consider when selecting a mutual fund that's right for you.

1. You have to compare the investment objective and risk tolerance of the fund with your objectives and investment comfort level. If you can't sleep at night because you are worrying about your hot stock fund losing money, then you should not own it. You should be investing in a conservative stock fund that gives you growth and income from dividends. Refer back to Chapter 1 to review the risk characteristics of both stock and bond funds.

2. You want to compare fees, commissions, and fund expenses. In the front of every prospectus is a section that shows you a hypothetical $1,000 investment and how it grows over 1, 5, and 10 years at 5 percent less fees, commissions, and fund expenses.

If you want to get more specific, you can compare each type of charge. You look at the front-end loads, back-end loads, 12b-1 sales distribution fees, and mutual fund management fees.

Irving Strauss, president of the 100 percent No-Load Mutual Fund Council in New York, advises investors to look at the front-end equivalent load of a fund that hits you with a 12b-1 charge.

"Loads and 12b-1 fees eat into your returns," says Strauss. "Over 10 years time, for example, a fund with a 1 percent 12b-1 fee would be the same as paying a 10 percent front-end load. Another way to look at it is to see how your money grows. If you invested $10,000 in a pure no-load fund earning 10 percent annually over 10 years, the money grows to $25,263. With a 1 percent 12b-1 charge, you are earning just 9 percent annually. The money grows to $23,674. The no-load advantage is $2,263."

You should also look at the mutual fund's expense ratio. That's how much the fund spends per the net asset value of the fund. The lower the expense ratio, the more money you have in your pocket. This is particularly important when selecting fixed-income or bond mutual funds. If the expense ratio is too high, it reduces the yield on your investment. It also reduces the amount of interest you can reinvest in the fund.

Table 5.1 shows some investment objective averages.

3. You have to evaluate the fund's performance or total return. A fund's total return includes price appreciation plus reinvestment of dividends and capital gains.

Irving Strauss says mutual fund investors should look at the following:

• *A fund's annual rate of return over at least a 1-, 3-, 5-, and 10-year period.*   The annual return is like the compound interest rate that you get with a bank CD. It shows you the rate your money grows, assuming that you earn money on your principal plus your earnings for the year.

• *A fund's yearly return over a number of time periods.*   You want to see from year to year how the fund has performed. You want a fund that shows consistent performance compared with other funds. You can have two funds that average 10 percent. One fund may earn 9 percent in year one and 11 percent in year two. The other fund may earn 15 percent in year one and 5 percent in year two. Both average 10 percent. But you want the

Table 5.1. Average Charges

Investment Objective Averages 06/30/92

No. of Funds	▶ Equity	Price/ Earnings Ratio(X)	Price/ Book Ratio(X)	Earnings Growth Rate %	Return On Assets %	Debt To Cap %	Market Cap $ Mil	% Cash Position	% Turnover Ratio	% Income Ratio	% Expense Ratio
44	Aggressive growth	22.4	4.5	18.9	8.8	22.3	1783	12.7	141	−0.40	1.84
34	Equity-income	17.9	2.8	7.1	6.0	35.0	7673	6.3	69	4.29	1.11
254	Growth	20.6	4.1	14.9	8.1	27.6	4735	11.8	101	1.20	1.33
125	Growth & income	18.5	3.3	9.7	6.9	32.2	7038	9.6	79	2.62	1.26
11	Europe stock	NM	NM	NM	NM	NM	17344	7.6	48	1.30	1.60
34	Foreign stock	11.6	1.9	NM	7.0	27.9	8369	9.0	67	1.10	1.69
11	Pacific stock	NM	NM	NM	NM	NM	NM	15.4	73	0.23	1.56
36	World stock	19.6	3.4	NM	6.7	28.2	6036	13.7	79	1.06	1.81
8	Specialty—financial	13.5	1.9	8.9	1.8	32.0	1392	3.4	141	1.39	1.66
9	Specialty—health	25.9	5.9	18.5	10.9	15.4	2188	10.5	96	0.21	1.36
14	Specialty—natural resources	21.6	2.5	5.3	5.3	33.9	3296	4.7	93	1.48	1.75
20	Specialty—precious metals	34.8	5.1	6.5	7.9	27.1	1862	12.6	51	1.10	1.65
14	Specialty—technology	23.5	5.3	23.6	12.5	10.9	1757	7.8	183	0.00	1.48
16	Specialty—utilities	15.1	1.9	3.6	4.3	49.2	6378	6.2	46	4.94	1.29
12	Specialty	21.2	3.5	11.7	7.0	32.0	1834	14.2	86	0.65	1.86
77	Small company	21.1	4.0	17.4	8.7	19.0	434	9.7	89	0.23	1.42

20	Asset allocation	19.4	3.2	9.7	7.0	30.4	6986	12.8	101	3.64	1.61
40	Balanced	19.4	3.6	10.6	7.3	31.1	6736	7.8	95	4.13	1.21
10	Income	16.6	2.2	11.7	5.3	40.6	5734	5.4	39	7.73	0.88
534	U.S. diversified equity fund average	20.1	3.8	13.8	7.8	27.5	4582	10.8	96	1.48	1.36
719	Equity fund average	20.5	3.8	13.7	7.7	27.8	4470	10.7	92	1.42	1.43
130	Hybrid fund average	19.0	3.3	10.4	8.3	62.0	3507	7.5	92	7.33	1.25

No. of Funds	▲ Fixed-Income	Avg. Weighted Maturity	Avg. Weighted Price	Avg. Weighted Coupon	% Cash Position	% Turnover Ratio	% Income Ratio	% Expense Ratio
14	Convertible bond	13.8	92.8	6.36	9.3	128	5.38	1.26
46	Corporate bond—high yield	8.6	96.2	11.49	4.1	87	12.22	1.19
36	Corporate bond—general	11.2	97.9	9.40	4.0	149	8.39	1.07
36	Corporate bond—high quality	10.2	101.0	8.53	9.5	114	7.64	0.81
13	Government bond—adj-rate mortgage	NM	100.3	7.24	32.1	231	6.86	0.94
57	Government Bond—general	13.5	101.6	8.69	6.5	204	7.78	1.16
35	Government Bond—mortgage	16.9	97.8	8.65	2.5	146	8.21	0.93
7	Government Bond—Treasury	9.0	91.4	8.18	1.9	110	6.82	0.61
17	World bond	8.2	60.1	9.16	10.9	211	7.89	1.56
17	Short-term world income	2.3	64.0	9.54	39.9	143	8.64	1.56
21	Municipal bond—California	21.9	101.0	7.13	4.2	40	6.29	0.67

(Continued)

Table 5.1. *(Continued)*

		Investment Objective Averages 06/30/92							
No. of Funds	▲ Fixed-Income	Avg. Weighted Maturity	Avg. Weighted Price	Avg. Weighted Coupon	% Cash Position	% Turnover Ratio	% Income Ratio	% Expense Ratio
99	Municipal bond—national	19.2	100.2	7.49	7.0	67	6.43	0.80
14	Municipal bond—New York	22.1	101.2	7.54	6.1	58	6.50	0.81
34	Municipal bond—single state	20.4	101.2	7.39	4.6	21	6.44	0.66
218	Taxable-bond fund average	12.5	93.7	8.78	8.9	162	7.92	1.08
168	Municipal-bond fund average	20.0	100.6	7.43	6.2	53	6.42	0.76

Source: Morningstar Mutual Fund Performance Report, Chicago. Used with permission.
Note: NM = Not meaningful.

consistent performer. You don't want a fund that shows wild price swings every year.

4. There are other things you will want to check out. These include:

• *A fund's performance in down markets.* This will tell you about the quality of the professional management. You want a consistent performer that loses less per month in down markets compared with other funds.

• *A fund's overall track record.* Table 5.2 will help you compare your fund with the peer group and market averages every year for the past 15 years (1971 through 1991), based on Morningstar Inc. data. If a fund has been around a long time, check its 1977 performance. The S&P 500 Stock index lost 7.44 percent that year.

Check the late 1970s and see how your taxable or *tax-free bond fund* performed compared with the bond fund averages. In 1979 and 1980, the Lehman Brothers Corporate Bond Index lost 2.11 percent and 0.29 percent, respectively. Tax-free funds also got hit hard during those years. National municipal bond funds lost 2.31 percent in 1978, 1.29 percent in 1979, and a whopping 11.32 percent in 1980. Also check more recent years. The S&P 500 Stock index lost 5.08 percent in 1980. In 1987, some fund categories lost a bundle, but the average equity fund was up less than 1 percent. In 1991, the S&P lost 3.1 percent, and the average equity fund lost 6.16 percent.

Bond funds have performed well over the past 10 years. Interest rates dropped from double-digit levels to between 4 percent and 8 percent, depending on the maturity of the bond. As a result, bond funds have grown at a staggering rate of 12.84 percent over the past 10 years ending in 1991.

tax-free bond fund: fund that invests in municipal bonds (Shareholders don't pay federal income taxes on municipal bond interest income. Investors in single-state municipal bond funds don't pay local, state, or federal taxes on the interest income from a municipal bond fund.)

bond funds: mutual funds that invest in fixed-income securities (Fund are distinguished by the type of securities—government or corporate, domestic or foreign—in the portfolio, the average maturity of the securities, and the credit quality of the issuer.)

Table 5.2. Group Performance

Investment Objective Annual Total Return Averages

	1977	1978	1979	1980	1981	1982	1983	1984	1985	1986	1987	1988	1989	1990	1991
EQUITY															
Aggressive growth	11.02	17.59	45.47	44.38	-5.95	26.55	18.77	-13.73	25.54	10.56	-2.69	14.98	26.07	-8.60	48.23
Equity-income	0.37	4.08	18.50	21.02	4.97	25.16	21.08	7.93	25.48	16.60	-1.55	16.06	21.08	-6.00	26.93
Growth	3.03	13.75	31.70	37.92	-1.41	26.74	20.96	-1.87	28.69	14.79	2.08	14.94	26.34	-5.71	36.13
Growth & income	-2.90	8.11	21.82	27.69	-0.43	23.19	21.27	4.01	27.24	15.21	1.55	14.76	23.33	-4.85	28.76
Small company	13.76	20.56	35.93	47.79	-1.25	29.63	26.33	-7.68	29.90	9.54	-1.98	19.20	23.27	-9.61	51.47
International—Europe stock	NA	NA	NA	NA	NA	NA	NA	NA	NA	17.17	10.12	8.26	23.13	-6.01	7.09
International—foreign stock	1.55	17.64	22.62	30.10	-2.56	4.95	27.83	-4.72	44.42	43.75	6.16	17.17	21.21	-11.92	12.27
International—Pacific stock	-5.72	54.84	-20.72	35.79	17.14	-2.65	35.14	-0.55	28.93	72.03	32.23	22.82	27.59	-19.71	11.74
International—world stock	2.27	17.73	31.74	37.17	-2.37	17.55	26.82	-5.81	40.00	30.95	5.46	13.52	21.14	-10.59	18.94
Specialty—financial	-2.11	9.91	21.67	6.40	20.18	18.08	29.03	16.74	42.32	14.94	-11.67	18.93	24.98	-14.88	60.64
Specialty—wealth	NA	NA	NA	NA	NA	45.34	6.11	-3.56	39.92	17.08	0.27	10.46	36.99	14.61	68.98
Specialty—miscellaneous	NA	NA	NA	NA	NA	NA	NA	NA	32.14	16.55	-2.79	24.62	22.55	-11.41	32.54
Specialty—natural resources	-4.00	12.07	59.75	56.09	-17.04	-10.90	20.48	-8.98	16.21	12.07	8.25	10.63	28.38	-8.54	6.96
Specialty—precious metals	31.82	9.21	164.27	64.10	-24.36	48.48	3.00	-25.39	-6.98	31.40	34.42	-15.81	23.22	-23.16	-4.43
Specialty—technology	0.76	16.97	30.24	38.83	-12.32	28.24	26.22	-9.73	18.01	6.08	1.00	4.46	22.49	-4.18	46.09
Specialty—utilities	8.60	-0.03	-0.42	4.09	11.89	22.62	11.83	18.91	26.80	21.00	-4.83	15.43	31.06	-3.53	20.51
HYBRID															
Asset allocation	NA	NA	NA	NA	NA	NA	NA	NA	13.61	16.97	10.70	7.89	16.64	-1.25	21.37
Balanced	0.42	4.46	15.95	19.85	3.30	29.10	17.89	7.03	27.58	17.66	2.41	11.76	18.34	-1.03	25.41
Convertible bond	3.64	5.52	15.92	26.77	1.60	28.68	19.16	2.01	23.13	14.82	-4.16	13.26	13.58	-6.20	30.27
Corporate bond—high yield	5.12	2.03	4.67	4.44	5.64	29.85	16.25	7.86	21.90	12.65	1.42	12.45	-1.31	-10.66	35.98
Income	5.89	4.66	12.99	15.57	8.25	27.74	15.37	8.67	20.39	12.41	-0.96	10.84	14.17	-0.81	23.65
World bond	NA	NA	NA	NA	NA	29.46	1.55	2.34	29.79	30.17	21.23	5.77	6.62	12.89	13.20

TAXABLE FIXED-INCOME

Corporate bond—general	4.85	1.58	0.62	1.68	4.63	32.70	9.14	12.66	21.42	14.09	2.18	8.82	10.45	5.70	16.70
Corporate bond—high quality	2.84	1.91	2.64	2.29	5.90	30.77	7.97	13.07	20.04	13.33	2.17	7.33	11.81	7.39	14.45
Government bond—adjustable rate mortgage	NA	NA	NA	NA	NA	NA	NA	NA	NA	8.37	-1.43	5.91	12.33	8.25	10.52
Government bond—general	1.20	3.18	2.01	3.98	6.39	29.39	7.51	13.26	17.41	11.98	1.36	6.52	11.80	8.09	13.91
Government bond—mortgage	2.83	-0.27	1.74	-2.41	5.52	29.39	8.35	13.30	19.11	11.20	2.25	7.39	12.53	9.43	14.42
Government bond—Treasury	NA	NA	NA	NA	10.64	18.04	6.16	12.66	17.34	24.78	0.05	8.82	14.82	6.74	14.86
Short-term world income	NA	NA	NA	NA	NA	NA	NA	NA	NA	NA	-9.35	10.26	-13.80	-0.57	6.39

TAX-FREE FIXED-INCOME

Municipal bond—California	NA	-1.59	-1.72	-10.05	-6.32	26.39	6.23	6.93	18.79	16.86	-2.36	10.90	9.60	6.57	10.96
Municipal bond—national	6.69	-2.31	-1.29	-11.32	-6.99	36.40	9.81	8.84	18.11	16.63	-0.19	10.44	9.23	6.12	11.34
Municipal bond—New York	NA	NA	NA	NA	NA	20.41	10.09	8.57	19.55	16.69	-1.79	10.64	9.25	5.16	12.84
Municipal bond—single state	NA	-2.95	-0.05	-19.13	-6.97	28.43	11.95	7.75	17.60	16.32	-1.26	11.41	9.45	6.02	11.34

SUMMARY

U.S. diversified equity fund average	2.63	12.39	29.48	35.13	-1.10	25.90	21.37	-1.48	28.02	14.04	0.90	15.50	24.77	-6.22	36.33
International equity fund average	1.32	25.11	18.48	34.26	1.00	9.07	28.39	-4.70	40.75	41.60	9.38	15.71	22.04	-11.75	13.91
Equity fund average	2.97	13.09	31.20	35.52	-1.60	24.78	21.29	-2.20	27.64	17.00	2.65	14.34	24.66	-7.42	31.56
Hybrid fund average	2.71	3.99	11.58	14.04	4.89	29.13	16.79	7.20	23.59	14.83	2.54	11.15	10.05	-2.50	26.09
Taxable fixed-income fund average	3.59	1.78	1.60	1.88	5.53	30.70	8.24	12.99	19.41	13.57	1.65	7.49	11.77	7.44	14.49
Tax-free fixed-income fund average	6.69	-2.31	-1.27	-11.67	-6.97	35.57	9.84	8.50	18.25	16.59	-0.96	10.86	9.35	6.05	11.45
Total fund average	3.11	9.34	22.28	24.03	-0.26	27.17	17.85	2.25	24.41	16.13	1.71	11.94	16.98	-1.03	23.14

(Continued)

Table 5.2. [Continued]

Investment Objective Annual Total Return Averages

	1977	1978	1979	1980	1981	1982	1983	1984	1985	1986	1987	1988	1989	1990	1991
INDEXES															
S&P 500 Index	-7.44	6.40	18.30	32.22	-5.08	21.46	22.46	6.13	31.64	18.63	5.22	16.51	31.67	-3.10	30.41
Lehman Bros Govt/Corp Bond Index	2.98	1.19	2.29	3.06	7.26	31.09	7.99	15.02	21.31	15.61	2.30	7.58	14.24	8.28	16.13
Lehman Bros Corporate Bond Index	3.16	0.36	-2.11	-0.29	2.95	39.20	9.27	16.62	24.06	16.53	2.56	9.22	13.98	7.15	18.51
Lehman Bros Government Bond Index	2.81	1.80	5.40	5.19	9.36	27.75	7.39	14.50	20.43	15.31	2.20	7.03	14.23	8.72	15.32
Lehman Bros Municipal Bond Index	NA	NA	NA	NA	-10.23	40.86	8.05	10.55	20.02	19.31	1.50	10.16	10.79	7.30	12.14
Morgan Stanley EAFE Index (net div)	18.06	32.62	4.75	22.58	-2.28	-1.86	23.69	7.38	56.16	69.44	24.63	28.27	10.54	-23.45	12.13
U S Treasury bills	5.26	7.22	10.04	11.58	14.01	10.70	8.62	9.57	7.49	5.97	5.83	6.67	8.11	7.51	5.41

Source: *Morningstar Mutual Fund Performance Report*, Chicago. Used with permission.

You won't see any negative yearly total return numbers for either taxable or tax-free bond funds over the past 10 years, so you have to check a couple of other factors when selecting bond funds:

• *The average maturity of a bond fund's portfolio.* The lower the average maturity the lower the price volatility.

• *The quality of the bonds in the portfolio.* Bond credit ratings are important. Bonds rated A to triple-A (AAA) by Standard & Poor's and Moody's Investors Services are issued by the most creditworthy corporations, so there is less chance that a default will lower the value of your portfolio. Of course, if you own a government securities bond fund, there is no risk of default. You face only interest-rate risk.

• *The bond fund's standard deviation in performance.* Standard deviation (SD) is a statistical term. It's the same as the margin of error you hear being discussed when the results of public opinion polls are announced—usually during political campaigns. For example, Candidate X may claim an estimated 51 percent of the vote if the election were held today, plus or minus 3 percentage points. The 3 percentage points is the margin of error, or standard deviation. It means that Candidate X's ratings could be as low as 48 percent or as high as 54 percent.

A bond fund's standard deviation is its margin of error. Robert Levy, president of CDA Technologies in Rockville, Maryland, says the SD highly correlates with how much the fund will gain or lose if interest rates rise or fall 1 percent. The SD tells you that two-thirds of the time a bond fund may swing 4 percentage points above or below its average return for the year. Say a bond fund shows a return of 6 percent for the year and has a SD of 2.5. You could expect to earn between about 3.5 percent and 8.5 percent for the year in the bond fund.

bond credit ratings: *a measure of a bond issuer's creditworthiness (Investment-grade bonds rated triple-A to single-A by Standard & Poor's and Moody's Investors Services are the safest. Low-rated or speculative bonds are considered junk bonds.)*

standard deviation: *the margin of error in a statistical forecast*

• *The length of time the manager has been running a fund.* Say a fund, whether a stock or bond fund, has a great 10-year track record. But this year the fund manager quit and a new one took over. Should you invest in the fund?

Sheldon Jacobs, publisher of the *No Load Investor*, says you should step back from the fund. You should see how the fund performs in both up and down markets and how it performs in relation to its peers before you invest.

• *The fund's portfolio turnover.* This will tell you whether the fund manager trades stocks or buys and holds for the long term. You will pay less taxes on funds with low portfolio turnover. High-turnover funds generate capital gains during bull markets. As a result, you pay more taxes on your mutual fund distributions, and the after-tax return on your fund is lower.

Figure 5.1 provides a checklist to help you rate a fund you are interested in buying.

SEEK EXPERT ADVICE

It's always good to get a second opinion when shopping for the mutual fund or funds that are right for you. Several highly regarded mutual fund newsletters on the market recommend funds. While each advisory letter takes a slightly different approach to mutual fund picking, all of the newsletter recommendations consider consistency of returns, fees and commissions, and performance. In addition, the newsletters provide you with recommended portfolios of funds based on your risk tolerance so that you can diversify your mutual investments to get the best returns with the least amount of risk.

The *No Load Investor*, published in Irvington-on-Hudson, New York, evaluates the performance of

Your objective: _____

Fund's objective: _____

Fund manager: _____

Length of time on the job: _____

Annual return over 1, 3, 5, and 10 years: _____

Consistency of returns every year (wide or narrow price swings): _____

Performance in down markets: _____

Front-end load: _____

12b-1 fee: _____

Back-end load: _____

Expense ratio: _____

Portfolio turnover %: _____

Figure 5.1. Mutual fund checklist.

more than 900 no-load mutual funds based on investment objective and current 1-, 3-, and 5-year performance figures. A one-volume almanac is also published annually. Sheldon Jacobs, editor and publisher, recommends funds based on their current performance and long-term track record. If a fund has a history of performing well and is currently showing strong performance relative to its peers, Jacobs recommends the fund. Jacobs uses trend indicators to determine which funds are likely to be the best investments.

Jacobs' recommendations don't change frequently. He tends to take a longer-term approach to mutual fund investing, so if you invest in one of his funds, you can buy and hold for the long term. Write the *No Load Investor*, P.O. Box 318, Irvington-on-Hudson, NY 10533, for more information.

Donoghue's Moneyletter, published in Ashland, Massachusetts, and *No Load Fund X*, published in San Francisco, recommend funds that show the best current performance trends. Both newsletters look at short-, intermediate-, and longer-term performance to come up with a composite rating. Current performance carries more weight than past performance when the ratings are calculated. When a recommended fund's performance starts slipping, the newsletters tell you to switch into better-performing funds.

Donoghue's Moneyletter and *No Load Fund X* use different formulas to determine recommended funds. The philosophy of the newsletters, however, is the same. You should always stay invested in the best-performing funds.

For more information, write *Donoghue's Moneyletter*, 290 Eliot Street, Box 91004, Ashland, MA 01721. The firm also publishes an annual almanac.

Contact *No Load Fund X* at 235 Montgomery Street, San Francisco, CA 94104.

Jay Schabacker's Mutual Fund Investing, published in Potomac, Maryland, takes a slightly different approach to picking funds. Editor Jay Schabacker uses a series of stock and bond market performance indicators to select the right funds. *Mutual Fund Investing,* like *Donoghue's Moneyletter* and *No Load Fund X,* tries to identify the top-performing funds. Schabacker gives investors buy and sell signals. So, if you go with his picks, be prepared to do a lot of telephone fund switching. Schabacker also publishes a quarterly performance report. For more information, write *Mutual Fund Investing,* 7811 Montrose Road, Potomac, MD 20854.

The Mutual Fund Letter, published by Dr. Gerald Perritt in Chicago, and *United Mutual Fund Selector,* published in Wellesley Hills, Massachusetts, take a long-term buy and hold approach to mutual fund investing. Both newsletters focus on consistency of performance. Perritt and UMF are not looking for the hot funds-of-the-month to trade. Perritt looks at the portfolio holdings of the funds he picks to make sure the holdings match the investment objectives and investment strategies of the fund. *United Mutual Fund Selector* compares the fund's performance with its peers and with the market over the long term. The newsletter editor wants to see high-ranking performance over both the past year and the longer term of 3 to 5 years.

Both the *Mutual Fund Letter* and *United Mutual Fund Selector* recommend funds that will live up to their investment objectives over the long term.

For more information, write the *Mutual Fund Letter,* 680 North Lake Shore Drive, Suite 2038, Chicago, IL 60611. Also available is a mutual fund encyclopedia that's updated annually.

The *United Mutual Fund Selector's* address is Babson United Building, 101 Prescott Street, Wellesley Hills, MA 02181.

The *Mutual Fund Forecaster* and *Income & Safety*, both published by the Institute of Econometric Research, Ft. Lauderdale, Florida, take a much different approach to selecting the best mutual funds. Their picks are based on mathematical research that looks at past performance to forecast fund equity returns over the coming year. You get 1-year profit projections on more than 1,000 stock funds. *Income & Safety*, a sister publication, also uses math to determine the best bond funds to invest in based on how much you would lose if interest rates dropped 1 percent. Remember, interest rates and bond prices move in opposite directions. The newsletter also looks at the yield and creditworthiness of funds' portfolios to come up with the best fixed-income funds to own.

Write the Institute of Econometric Research, 3471 North Federal Highway, Ft. Lauderdale, FL 33306, for more information.

Morningstar Mutual Funds of Chicago is another useful publication that is available in most public libraries. The monthly publication keeps tabs on over 3,000 stock and bond funds. You get risk and return ratings, fees, portfolio holdings, and commentary on the funds. Morningstar gives funds a one- to five-star rating. One is the worst and five is the best. The star rating indicates how a fund ranks against similar funds in both up and down markets. For more information, write Morningstar, 53 West Jackson Blvd., Chicago, IL 60604. Morningstar also publishes an annual source book and monthly performance reports.

PART 2

THE FUNDS

CHAPTER 6

Aggressive Growth
and Small-Company
Stock Funds

The names of these two fund classes tell it all. Aggressive growth and small-company stock funds are high-performance funds. Although there are slight differences between the two fund groups, their investment objectives are the same—capital appreciation.

Aggressive growth funds and small-company funds can be big winners in some years and big losers in others, so the funds are not for the faint of heart. Investors who are looking for long-term growth and who are willing to tolerate short-term losses should consider these funds.

For example, aggressive growth funds gained a whopping 49.7 percent in 1991, according to Morningstar Inc.'s data. Small-company stock funds racked up 52.6 percent gains in the same year.

Over the past 15 years, ending in May 1992, aggressive growth funds grew at an annual rate of 15.4 percent. Small-company funds grew 16.3 percent annually over the same period.

Sounds great. Before you empty your savings account in quest of big mutual fund profits, keep in mind that you can lose a lot of money over the short haul. For example, in 1984 you lost 12.9 percent and 7 percent in aggressive growth funds and small-company funds, respectively. Funds that invested for growth got hit much harder in 1974, however. The average fund lost 27 percent. And in October of 1987, the average aggressive fund lost a whopping 26 percent.

Although these funds are volatile performers, they fit well in a portfolio of mutual funds that includes more conservative stock funds, bond funds, and money funds. Chapter 13 will show you how to construct a mix of funds that gives you the best returns with the least amount of risk based on your tolerance for risk.

In a nutshell, it works this way: In up markets, you pick up large gains in small-company or aggressive funds. In down markets, your losses are hedged by holding money funds and bond funds. While you will not make as much as a 100 percent stake in these aggressive-type stock funds, you may earn 80 percent of the return with half the risk.

AGGRESSIVE GROWTH FUNDS

aggressive growth fund: a high-risk fund that invests for maximum capital appreciation

Aggressive growth funds invest in both large and small companies. The stocks may be traded on the New York Stock Exchange, the American Stock Exchange, or the over-the-counter stock market, which lists on the National Association of Securities Dealers Automated Quotation system known as NASDAQ.

The typical stock held by an aggressive growth fund has a market capitalization of $2.1 billion. By contrast, the market capitalization of small-company funds is under $500 million. Market capitalization is a term that indicates the value of the number of shares issued by a company that is traded on the stock exchanges. The market capitalization of the Vanguard Index 500, an index fund that holds all the stocks that make up the S&P 500, has a market capitalization of $11 billion. So you can see that most of the stocks held by aggressive funds are quite small.

The small size of both aggressive growth and small-company stock fund holdings is the reason for big swings in their performance. Small stocks are thinly traded. There are not as many buys and sells of these stocks compared with stocks that trade on the New York Stock Exchange. Thin volume means that when there is a big buyer or several big buyers, the price of these stocks gets driven up fast.

Many small stocks are also lower-priced stocks. For example, a $2 change in a $10 stock translates into a 20 percent gain or loss. By contrast, a $2 change in a $40 stock is just a 5 percent change in value.

Aggressive stock fund portfolio managers are looking for profits. They may go for home runs or extra base hits instead of hitting singles. The fund managers may speculate on thinly traded, overlooked stocks in hopes of making big gains. They may also boost returns by trading options, selling stocks short, and buying on margin. Aggressive growth fund portfolio managers will own stocks in large companies like Philip Morris, with over $6 billion in sales, because the firm is expected to have strong earnings and profits in the future. At this writing, aggressive stock fund managers own smaller-sized companies like Helig Meyers, a successful furniture store chain that operates in smaller towns in the Southeast. The stock trades on the New York Stock Exchange. The firm's revenues are expected to grow to $675 million by year-end 1993, up from $520 million in 1991. The firm's earnings are also expected to grow at about a 17 percent annual rate over the next few years.

By contrast, small-company stock funds own a stake in emerging companies. The stocks are traded on the NASDAQ or over-the-counter stock exchange. For example, Synergen, Inc., is one of the most widely held small-company fund holdings. This biotechnology firm, which is traded on the NASDAQ stock exchange, is making drugs to treat arthritis and ulcers. Revenues are expected to grow to $20 million by year-end 1993, up from $14 million in 1991. If Synergen's drugs are successfully tested and approved for sale by the Federal Drug Administration, earnings are expected to grow at double-digit rates.

Table 6.1 lists leading aggressive growth funds; Table 6.2 shows the top 25 small-company stock fund holdings.

SMALL-COMPANY STOCK FUNDS

A fine line of difference exists between aggressive growth stock funds and small-company stock funds. *Small-company stock funds* invest in smaller firms than do aggressive growth funds. In addition, small-company stock funds tend to be slightly less volatile than aggressive growth funds. According to *Morningstar Mutual Funds*, the average small-company fund sports a *beta value* of 1.09, compared with 1.19 for aggressive growth funds. The S&P 500 Stock index has a beta value of 1, so small-company stocks would move 1.09 times the percent gain or loss on the S&P 500. Aggressive growth funds would move about 1.19 times the gain or loss on the S&P 500.

Over the past six decades, small-company stock funds have grown at an annual rate of 12 percent, according to Ibbotson Associates data. In any given year, the price swing is about 31 percent, so you

small-company stock funds: funds that invest in stocks sold on the over-the-counter stock market

beta value: a statistical measure of risk that tells you how much a fund or security moves in relation to the market (The S&P 500 has a beta value of 1.)

Table 6.1. Aggressive Growth Funds

| Portfolio | | | Top 25 Holdings | |
Share Change	Amount 000	Stock	Value $000	% Net Assets
	924	Home Depot	60545	0.80
	1359	Novell	76279	0.59
	1071	Amgen	67436	0.56
	1184	Cisco Systems	51371	0.54
	687	Philip Morris	52100	0.54
	1031	Intel	58219	0.53
	587	Microsoft	54776	0.51
	1283	Intl Game Technology	40098	0.50
	523	US Surgical	53485	0.44
	525	Medtronic	42288	0.41
	97	IBM	9245	0.39
	778	Benguet Cl B	778	0.36
	218	Loewen Group	2942	0.35
	1192	Office Depot	34421	0.35
	733	Wal-Mart Stores	39770	0.35
	48	CPAC	380	0.34
	306	FNMA	19497	0.34
	841	Circus Circus Enterprises	35455	0.33
	536	Pfizer	38659	0.33
	668	Countrywide Credit Industry	22325	0.32
	6041	Gulf States Utilities	84621	0.32
	439	Merck	43582	0.32
	676	US Healthcare	32728	0.32
	1038	Brinker International	36459	0.31
	669	Chiron	35530	0.30

Source: Morningstar Mutual Funds, Chicago. Used with permission.

run about a 68 percent chance of losing 19 percent or making 43 percent in any given year. Over the long term, however, you will average about 12 percent.

There's overwhelming evidence that small-

Table 6.2. Small-Company Stock Fund Holdings

Portfolio			Top 25 Holdings	
Share Change	Amount 000	Stock	Value $000	% Net Assets
	1517	Novell	87684	0.49
	3176	Cisco Systems	153133	0.46
	1471	BMC Software	88096	0.39
	2693	Amgen	167821	0.37
	1687	Microsoft	162414	0.35
	1864	CUC International	51600	0.34
	1279	Office Depot	53947	0.32
	3386	Medco Containment Services	202837	0.31
	1431	Saint Jude Medical	72360	0.31
	1669	Symantec	60795	0.29
	1447	Genzyme	73867	0.27
	1196	Parametric Technology	42900	0.26
	1247	Anthem Electronics	51165	0.25
	1517	United Healthcare	102640	0.25
	611	Heilig-Meyers	21188	0.24
	1066	Critical Care America	51968	0.23
	362	Mirage Resorts	12251	0.23
	1389	US Surgical	133852	0.23
	547	CML Group	18770	0.22
	2173	Continental Medical Systems	55462	0.22
	2078	Novacare	50722	0.22
	506	Score Board	14970	0.22
	1253	Perrigo	40342	0.21
	1630	Synergen	88078	0.21
	959	Vivra	28762	0.21

Source: Morningstar Mutual Funds, Chicago. Used with permission.

company stock funds or aggressive growth funds belong in most investors' portfolios. But don't bet the ranch on hot stock funds that can double in a year. Asset allocation experts say it is better to pepper portfolios with a few well-managed equity funds that invest in over-the-counter stocks. That way you can enhance the risk-adjusted rate of return on the investments.

There's a strong case to be made for small-company stock fund investing. Statistics published by Ibbotson Associates indicate that investing in small-company stock funds is a good bet for the long term. For example:

• Small-company stocks have registered 12 percent annual returns compared with 10 percent annual returns on the S&P 500 over the last 6 decades.

• In every period immediately following a recession since 1954, small-company stocks have outperformed large-company stocks in the ensuing 12 months.

• Small-company stocks exhibit a pattern of leading and lagging the S&P 500 Stock index for several years at a time. For example, they outpaced the S&P 500 from 1961 through 1968 then fell behind for eight years. Small-company stocks then beat the broad market from 1974 through 1983. Large-company stocks outpaced their smaller cousins for the next 7 years. But now small-company stocks are up 40 percent year-to-date ending in mid-November 1991.

• Small-company stocks can enhance the performance of a portfolio of large-company stocks. Small stocks outperformed the S&P 500 in 4 out of the last 5 decades.

Today the money is flowing into small stocks. Could this be a harbinger for higher returns in small-company stock funds over the next few years? Only time will tell. But according to the Securities Industry Association, trading by individual investors is up 18 percent over last year. The beneficiaries are small-company stocks. Trading volume on NASDAQ is averaging 160 million shares daily, compared with 149 million shares 5 years ago.

Although small-company stocks funds were up a whopping 60 percent on average over the past 12 months ending in October 1991, net asset values are starting to fall back because of profit taking and the continuing recession. But fund managers are optimistic for the long haul.

The portfolio management strategies of small-company stock funds differ. Some funds invest based on earnings growth trends. Others want to buy overlooked companies that are not followed by many analysts on Wall Street. The fund managers want to buy stocks whose price is cheaper in relation to earnings than those of other small-company stocks. In other words, they want to own stocks with low price-to-earnings (P/E) ratios. Binkly Shorts, manager of the OTC Securities Fund, believes small-company stocks will continue to outpace the broad market over the next several years. He's looking for an expected rate of return on his fund of 14 percent over the next year, but he is cautious:

"I don't pretend like I'm going to do that," says Shorts, whose fund is up 35 percent this year. "I think small company stocks will continue to do well. The real values are at the lower end of the market capitalization range. Earnings are growing faster than large company stocks. But the biggest problem small firms face is access to capital. Banks are not lending. It is causing dramatic problems and could continue to do so."

Others agree. Lawrence Auriana, comanager of the Kaufman Fund, says he's investing in "emerging growth companies that have solid profitability, strong growth prospects and proprietary technologies that result in leading market positions."

John Ballen, manager of MFS Emerging Growth Fund, is looking for more explosive growth after the country pulls out of this nagging recession.

"Coming out of the recession, you will have accelerating earnings with the small caps," says Ballen. "The ratio of stock prices to earnings or the P/E multiple should expand and provide for good opportunities in the emerging growth stock market."

FUND MANAGERS DIFFER IN INVESTMENT STYLE

Aggressive growth and small-company funds are not all alike, even though the fund managers all look for big profits. Take the AIM Constellation Fund, the top-performing aggressive growth fund over the past 10 years ending in May 1992, according to *Morningstar Mutual Funds*. The fund has grown at an annual rate of 20.5 percent over the past 10 years. For the current year-to-date, however, the fund is down 4.6 percent.

AIM buys both small- and medium-sized emerging growth companies. The fund managers evaluate stocks based on earnings growth rates and stock price trends. The managers also like to buy undervalued stocks—underpriced stocks in relation to a company's earnings. The managers also look for special situations and will trade stocks for short-term profits. As a result, the fund has a high portfolio turnover rate.

In 1991, the fund gained 70 percent as a result of the bull market in small-company stocks. The fund managers outperformed the average aggressive growth fund by 30.45 percentage points because they invested in stocks with strong earnings growth rates. The average five-year earnings growth rate of the stock held in the AIM portfolio stands at 24.6 percent at this writing.

The Alliance Quasar Fund, up 15.61 percent over the past 10 years ending in May 1992, takes a different approach to aggressive growth stock investing. Rather than trade for quick profits based on a firm's earnings, the fund manager looks for values. He wants to buy undervalued stock—overlooked stocks whose prices don't reflect their potential earnings. The fund manager also looks at the economy and what industries will perform well under different economic conditions. For example, the fund profited handsomely from its stake in the technology sector of the economy.

Founders Special Fund is a successful small-company stock fund. Over the past 10 years, the fund grew at an annual rate of 17.49 percent. The fund invests in small companies that exhibit favorable sales and earnings growth trends. The fund may also buy larger out-of-favor stocks in companies whose fortunes they hope will improve. The fund is characterized by high portfolio turnover. In addition, the fund manager likes to buy stocks that have been beaten down in price. In April 1992, the fund increased its position in health care and biotechnology stocks after stocks in these industries declined due to a correction.

By contrast, the Acorn Fund, which grew at an 18.55 percent annual rate over the past 10 years ending in June 1992, takes a different approach to small stock fund investing. The fund buys and holds small-company stocks for an average of 3 to 5 years. The manager also uses the value-oriented method of stock picking. Stocks are selected depending on whether they are underpriced based on their earnings. The companies are expected to be financially strong and are not widely followed by institutional investors. The fund profits when

Table 6.3. Leading Aggressive Growth Funds
6/30/92

		5 Years		
Net Assets 03/31/92	Name	TR% 5 Yr	Rank All	Obj
186.2	Kaufmann	15.03	27	1
115.9	Thomson Opportunity B	14.71	31	2
59.7	Keystone America Omega	12.96	51	3
292.3	Founders Special	12.65	60	4
69.5	Equity Strategies	12.36	68	5
725.9	AIM Constellation	12.31	70	6
1384.0	Putnam Voyager A	12.14	76	7
129.6	Delaware Group Trend	11.80	91	8
110.0	MetLife-State Street Capital Apprec	10.80	157	9
159.0	Pacific Horizon Aggressive Growth	10.08	254	10
1060.0	Fidelity Capital Appreciation	9.72	349	11
163.8	Seligman Capital	9.20	513	12
28.0	ABT Emerging Growth	9.18	520	13
12.0	Wasatch Aggressive Equity	8.57	731	14
198.2	Shearson Aggressive Growth	8.40	776	15
77.2	Nicholas-Applegate Growth Equity A	8.28	825	16
31.0	SunAmerica Aggressive Growth	8.20	849	17
56.0	Dreyfus Strategic Aggressive Invstg	7.84	929	18
17.7	AIM Aggressive Growth(C)	7.80	940	19
356.1	Oppenheimer Target	7.77	949	20
	Avg. Annual Return / # of Funds	6.87		42

Source: Morningstar Mutual Fund Performance Report, Chicago. Used with permission.
Note: TR% is the total return percentage over the indicated period. Total returns over 5 years are annualized.

the stocks become popular and investors start buying them.

Table 6.3 shows the top 20 performing aggressive growth funds over the past 5 years, and Table 6.4 shows the top small-company funds. Past per-

**Table 6.4.   Leading Small-Company Funds
6/30/92**

	5 Years			
Net Assets 03/31/92	Name	TR% 5 Yr	Rank All	Obj
113.3	Founders Frontier	17.21	8	1
3775.9	Twentieth Century Ultra Investors	15.60	19	2
114.8	Alger Small Capitalization	15.08	25	3
1530.7	Janus Venture	14.92	30	4
53.4	Skyline Special Equities	13.65	42	5
179.1	Nicholas Limited Edition	13.06	49	6
262.7	Calvert-Ariel Growth	12.64	61	7
242.1	Oppenheimer Discovery	12.51	62	8
109.6	FPA Capital	12.42	65	9
19.7	FAM Value	12.40	66	10
316.5	Columbia Special	12.34	69	11
1133.4	Fidelity OTC	12.28	72	12
66.2	Twentieth Century Giftrust Investors	12.22	75	13
18.8	Meridian	11.61	99	14
43.3	Managers Special Equity	11.55	104	15
48.0	Baron Asset	11.39	111	16
1255.5	Acorn	11.07	140	17
149.6	Hartwell Emerging Growth	11.04	142	18
254.9	Sit "New Beginning" Growth.	10.45	195	19
257.4	MFS Lifetime Emerging Growth	10.36	206	20
	Avg. Annual Return / # of Funds	8.44		

Source: Morningstar Mutual Fund Performance Report, Chicago.
Used with permission.
Note: TR% is the total return percentage over the indicated period.
Total returns over 5 years are annualized.

formance, however, is no indication of future results. When looking for an aggressive growth or small-company fund, check a fund's past performance each year and see how the fund ranks in performance compared with its peers. Look for consistent performance. Check the industry concentration and stock holdings of the fund. A manager may be betting on a couple of industries or out-of-favor stocks, a strategy that you may or may not agree with.

AGGRESSIVE AND SMALL-STOCK FUNDS ARE RISKY: A REMINDER

You have to be willing to accept short-term losses in return for long-term gains when you invest in these types of mutual funds. Data show that you have to own these funds for at least a decade to make the risk work for and not against you.

For example, small stocks were up at an annual rate of 20.7 percent in the decade of the 1940s. They also outpaced the S&P 500 in the 1960s and 1970s. They lagged behind the broad-based market in the 1980s and lost almost 22 percent in 1990. But near the tail end of 1991, the NASDAQ year-to-date earnings are up 45 percent compared with 14 percent for the S&P 500.

When shopping for an aggressive or small-company stock fund, adhere to the following rules before you invest:

- Check for consistent returns from year to year. You don't want to invest in funds with wide performance swings.
- Check how the fund did during down periods like 1981, 1984, October 1987, and 1990. You want funds with high annual returns that lost the least on the downside.

- Check the financial condition and prospects of the stocks in the portfolio. Sources of information on small stocks include *Moody's OTC Industrial Manual* and *Standard & Poor's Stock Reports*.
- Check the fund's expense ratio. You want the fund with the lowest expenses so you will earn more money.
- Check the loads and 12b-1 charges. You don't want to get gouged by your stockbroker or financial planner.
- Check the size of the fund and the median market capitalization of its holdings. Funds with assets under $100 or $200 million have greater trading flexibility than billion dollar growth stock funds. You also get a bigger bang for your buck—as well as more risk—when you invest in small firms with market capitalizations of under $500 million.

HOW MUCH SHOULD YOU INVEST?

How much should you invest in aggressive or small-company stocks? A lot depends, of course, on your tolerance for risk. If you are willing to accept some short-term losses in return for long-term gains, then you should keep a hand in the small-company stock market. If you are willing to mix small-company stock funds with growth and income funds, money funds, and precious metals funds as an inflation hedge, you can sleep at night knowing your investments are well diversified.

Because of the lingering recession, Morton Silverman, chief investment officer at Piper Jaffray & Hopewood in Minneapolis, encourages investors to play it safe with their asset allocation mixes. He has predicted that expected rates of return on stocks, bonds, and cash will be below recent historical levels.

For example, for the next one to four years, his

forecast calls for the following expected rates of return: cash, 5.5 percent; fixed income, 8.2 percent; U.S. common stocks, 9.9 percent; international common stocks, 11.7 percent; and inflation hedges, 1.8 percent.

"We think the returns of the 1990s could be less than the 1980s," says Silverman. "The timing of the economic turnaround remains in doubt. The consumer lacks confidence. Corporate earnings will be improving, but will be well below our recovery experience of recent years. There will be little progress made in fixing the federal budget deficit."

Silverman is advising investors to play it safe when they allocate assets. He recommends the following mixes:

• *Building for retirement:* 25 percent fixed income, 25 percent international stock fund, 10 percent cash, 5 percent inflation hedges, 9 percent small-company stocks, and 26 percent blue-chip stocks.

• *Education and estate planning:* 20 percent fixed income, 25 percent international stock fund, 10 percent cash, 5 percent inflation hedges, 10 percent small-company stocks, and 30 percent blue-chip stocks.

• *Total-return-oriented retirees:* 30 percent fixed income, 25 percent international stock fund, 10 percent cash, 5 percent inflation hedges, 8 percent small-company stocks, and 22 percent blue-chip stocks.

CHAPTER 7

Growth and Income Stock Funds

There are two ways to invest for long-term growth. One way is to invest in growth stock mutual funds. The other way is to invest in growth-and-income mutual funds.

Growth funds invest for long-term growth by investing in large-company stocks that should appreciate in value. Growth-and-income funds also invest for growth but have a secondary objective of providing investors with income from dividends.

Over the past 3, 5, and 10 years, there has not been much difference in the performance of growth and growth-and-income funds. According to Morningstar Inc., growth funds have grown at annual rates of return of 10.64 percent, 8.43 percent, and 15.86 percent, respectively, over the past 3, 5, and 10 years ending in June 1992. By contrast, growth-and-income funds grew at 10.18 percent, 8.27 percent, and 15.78 percent over the past 3, 5, and 10 years, respectively.

Whether you invest in growth or growth-and-income funds depends on your preference for dividend income. Growth-and-income funds invest in high-yielding stocks and fixed-income securities. So when you own a growth-and-income fund, you get some of the companies' profits returned to you in the form of dividends. By contrast, growth funds own stocks that pay little or no dividends—you get your profits from the price appreciation of the stocks.

GROWTH FUNDS

Growth funds are less aggressive than small-company stock funds but more aggressive than high-yielding growth-and-income funds.

growth funds: funds that invest in well-seasoned companies for long-term growth

Obviously, the funds invest in growth stocks. The funds buy stocks in larger firms traded on the New York, American, and NASDAQ stock exchanges. The average market capitalization of stocks owned by growth funds is $4.95 billion. The companies are considered growth companies for a couple of important reasons:

- The companies are dominant players in their industries. They are expected to gain a greater market share of their products.
- The companies are well managed. The firms have high profit margins and are expected to show strong revenue and profit growth over the next several years.
- The firms are expected to show double-digit earnings growth rates.

In essence, when you invest in a fund that buys growth stocks, you are buying a fund whose portfolio manager expects to see a company's earnings and dividends grow faster than the overall economy.

And how does a company do that? Growth fund portfolio managers use several different financial calculations to arrive at a firm's earnings growth rate. For example, they look at a company's return on equity (ROE). ROE is the rate of return the company is earning on the value of the shareholder's stock or equity. In addition, the fund manager wants to see how much money the company's management is plowing back into the company. The manager wants to see if a substantial amount of a company's profits are being reinvested in, for example, new plant and equipment, new products, research and development, and marketing.

The manager is looking at the firm's retention rate, or earnings less dividends paid out divided by the firm's earnings. The higher the rate, the more money is going into growing the company.

Here's a simplified version of how it works. Say a company has a return on equity of 18 percent and a retention rate of 80 percent: The firm's growth rate is 0.18 times 0.80 or 14.4 percent.

Fast-growing companies, however, can go in and out of favor on Wall Street. You can get big gains or big losses in growth stock mutual funds. According to *CDA/Wiesenberger's Mutual Fund Update*, the average growth fund gained 15.3 percent a year over the past 10 years ending in June 1992. The highest return was 23.8 percent and the lowest was −11.3 percent.

The beta value of growth funds is also higher than 1. A beta value of 1 is considered the market average. Beta measures how a fund moves in relation to the market. A fund with a beta of 1.05 would move up or down about 5 percent more than the S&P 500 Stock index. The higher the beta, the greater the volatility of the fund. Currently, growth funds sport a beta of 1.01, which is slightly higher than the market average but lower than the 1.08 beta value on aggressive growth stock funds.

When you invest in a growth stock fund, or any type of aggressive fund for that matter, you expect to earn more than the stock market in good years and lose more than the stock market in bad years. Hopefully, however, the longer you own a growth fund the more your gains will outweigh your losses.

When you put your hard-earned cash in a growth fund, here are some of the typical stocks you may own, according to *Morningstar Mutual Funds*.

Walt Disney, an entertainment company that trades on the New York Stock Exchange, is expected to have almost $9 billion in revenues by year-end 1993. The stock has a dividend yield of just 0.6 percent (six-tenths of 1 percent). Earnings at Disney are expected to grow at close to a 16 percent annual rate over the next few years.

Wal-Mart Stores, the popular and largest retail group of stores in the nation, is expected to have $68 billion in sales by year-end 1993, up from $44 billion in 1991. The stock yields just 0.4 percent. Earnings are growing at almost 19 percent a year.

A list of the 25 largest growth fund holdings is shown in Table 7.1.

Growth Fund Management Styles Differ

Not all growth stock fund managers invest based on a company's expected earnings growth rate. Some fund managers buy stocks based on value. *Value investing* is when a fund buys underpriced stock with good prospects. Everyone wants to own mutual funds that invest in undervalued and overlooked stocks. It makes a good story. Value-oriented mutual funds buy firms with strong balance sheets whose stocks are cheap compared with the market and their peer group. Value funds often own companies whose breakup value per share or private market value per share is more than the current price per share.

By contrast, earnings momentum funds fre-

value investing: when a fund buys underpriced stocks that have the potential to perform well

Table 7.1. Growth Fund Holdings

Portfolio			Top 25 Holdings	
Share Change	Amount 000	Stock	Value $000	% Net Assets
	37227	Philip Morris	2813635	1.53
	35882	FNMA	2302246	0.96
	10656	Merck	1269106	0.83
	9998	Bristol-Myers Squibb	797194	0.81
	22125	Pfizer	1624836	0.77
	28779	Wal-Mart Stores	1497801	0.75
	12469	General Electric	762097	0.63
	7565	Johnson & Johnson	630451	0.61
	8178	FHLMC	831601	0.55
	11608	Intel	627597	0.54
	9682	Microsoft	972743	0.54
	13458	Home Depot	864515	0.52
	15728	Pepsico	542626	0.48
	10554	Abbott Laboratories	583489	0.47
	14041	Waste Management	520567	0.47
	18169	Amgen	1128658	0.44
	10229	Coca-Cola	644019	0.43
	11496	Gillette	545873	0.43
	14692	Novell	793468	0.43
	5850	IBM	530058	0.39
	10211	SLMA	671053	0.39
	12518	Toys 'R' Us	403673	0.39
	14373	Glaxo Holdings	522200	0.37
	7945	Schlumberger	489242	0.37
	18574	Telefonos de Mexico	545265	0.37

Source: Morningstar Mutual Funds, Chicago. Used with permission.

quently look at a firm's recent two to three quarters of earnings performance in relation to the company's historical rate of growth. Earnings momentum funds like the 20th Century Growth Fund, up 24.73 percent annually over the past 3 years ending in March 1992, according to Morningstar Inc., ride the trends of rising profitability, while growth funds, such as the Kemper Growth Fund, up 25.84 percent annually over the past 3 years, buy companies that are expected to show strong earnings growth over the longer term.

According to the *L/G No Load Fund Analyst*, a San Francisco–based newsletter, value funds grew at an annual rate of 11.4 percent over the 3 years ending in 1991. By contrast, funds that invested based on earnings momentum grew at a 28.7 annual rate. Long-term growth funds gained 20.3 percent annually while the S&P 500 grew 18.4 percent annually.

Value funds had their heyday in the 1980s. Funds that bought cheap before and during the bull market—for example, funds like the Gabelli Asset Fund, Windsor Fund, Mutual Series, and Lindner Dividend and Lindner Fund—performed well. As a group, these funds outpaced the other types of funds by more than 1 to 3 percentage points in annual return for three years ending in 1988, according to the *L/G No Load Fund Analyst*.

Have value funds lost their touch since the 1980s?

Many analysts say no, and advise investors to own both a value and growth-oriented stock fund.

Ken Gregory, editor of the *L/G No Load Fund Analyst*, says stock-picking styles run in cycles. By the end of March 1992, value funds were up 4.1 percent on average compared with −1.2 percent for long-term growth funds and −3.9 percent for earnings momentum funds. But over the next 12 months, growth funds will be the winners.

"Value funds may continue to outperform for several months at a time," says Gregory, "but growth stocks as a group continue to be reasonably priced relative to the overall market. The sluggish recovery will favor growth over value. Value funds will perform well when others jump on the bandwagon and buy undervalued stocks."

Michael Lipper, president of Lipper Analytical Services in New York, agrees. He says that when there is a big performance gap between growth-oriented and value-oriented mutual funds, the gap tends to narrow. As a result, value funds have been gaining ground on growth funds this year.

Typically, reports the *United Mutual Fund Selector*, a Massachusetts-based mutual fund newsletter, value stocks tend to "beat the overall market at the end of recessions and in the early stages of an economic recovery." Growth-oriented funds tend to perform better when the economy gets rolling.

It's hard to decide which type of growth fund to own—one that looks for high earnings growth rates or one that looks for undervalued companies.

The *United Mutual Fund Selector* favors some of the following funds with good long-term track records:

• AIM Weingarten has grown at an annual rate of 20.4 percent over the past 10 years, although it was down 11 percent by the end of June 1992. The fund invests based on earnings momentum. However, the stocks must show sustained growth and have earnings that outpace what analysts have forecasted in their brokerage firm reports.

• Gabelli Growth is a newer fund that has grown at a 22.8 percent annual rate over the past 3 years ending in June 1992. The fund manager likes to buy cheap stocks that sell at low prices in relation to earnings and that are expected to show strong earnings growth rates.

• Growth Fund of America dropped 4.3 percent in the first 6 months of 1992 but has an annual growth rate of 16.6 percent over the past 10 years. Like other growth fund investors, the manager of the fund looks for stocks likely to show high earnings growth rates.

• IAI Regional Fund is a growth fund that invests 80 percent of assets in midwestern companies. The fund was up 19.2 percent annually for the 10 years ending in 1991 but moved down during the first half of 1992. The fund buys blue-chip stocks and medium-sized stocks that have strong earnings growth rates.

• Nicholas Fund is a growth fund that buys and holds undervalued growth companies for the long term. The fund is down just 1 percent through June 1992. Over the past 10 years, the fund grew at a 17.6 percent annual rate.

Despite the stellar performance of growth stock mutual funds, Ken Gregory thinks investors should keep 30 percent of their stock fund portfolio in value-oriented funds. Two funds he now favors because the fund managers "are more dynamic in their search for value" are Gabelli Asset Fund and Southeastern Asset Management Value.

The Gabelli Asset Fund, which was up 12.2 percent annually over the past three years ending in 1991, buys stock in firms that sell below the private market value of the firm. Private market value is a company's selling price if it were to be sold. The manager also looks at strong cash flow and long-term earnings trends.

The Southeastern Asset Management Value Trust, which is up 12.2 percent annually over the past 3 years, looks for cheap stocks. The fund buys stocks of companies selling at discounts of at least 50 percent to their private business worth or a firm's liquidating value. The fund manager also looks at potential earnings growth for at least 2 years, a strong balance sheet, and excess cash flow. The fund holds 20 to 30 stocks in the portfolio for the longer term—from 2 to 5 years.

GROWTH-AND-INCOME FUNDS

What about your old-fashioned conservative stock funds?

Despite all the sexy stories fund managers tell about undervalued stocks or companies with fantastic earnings forecasts, there's something to be said for investing in high-quality, large-capitalization (large-cap) stocks that pay good dividends.

growth-and-income funds: funds that invest for both capital appreciation and income

That's the secret of *growth-and-income funds*. At this writing, growth-and-income funds have recorded yields ranging from 2.5 percent to 6 percent. When you buy a growth-and-income fund, you own high-quality blue-chip stocks that pay high dividend yields. You get growth from the stocks; you collect profits in hand from the company, which serves to cushion stock market losses; and you can reinvest those juicy dividends in more shares.

Steve Norwitz, spokesperson for T. Rowe Price, a Baltimore-based mutual fund company with assets of more than $20 billion under management, says reinvesting and compounding of dividends boost returns over the long term. According to Standard & Poor's statistics, more than 40 percent of the S&P 500's total return in the past 10 years is due to reinvested dividends. Dividends accounted for 7.2 percentage points of the market's 18 percent annual return on the broad market over the past 10 years ending in March 1992.

CDA/Wiesenberger's data show that the average growth-and-income funds, up 15 percent annually over the past 10 years, provided investors with solid returns at less risk than growth or aggressive growth funds. Growth-and-income funds sport beta values of 0.81, so they are less volatile than the S&P 500, aggressive growth, or growth funds.

Growth-and-income funds hit a high return of 19.4 percent and a low of −1.0 percent over the past 10 years.

A range of 19.4 and −1.0 for growth-and-income funds is a lot easier to take than the 23.8 and −11.3 percent range of return on growth funds.

Growth-and-income funds or their higher-yielding second cousins, equity income funds, buy stocks of well-seasoned companies that pay high dividend yields. The fund managers, however, also want capital appreciation. So, like their growth fund cousins, they try to find large companies that are expected to show strong earnings growth rates compared with their peers, or they buy stocks that are considered undervalued based on the price of the stock in relation to the company's current or future earnings.

Exxon and AT&T are typical stocks owned by growth-and-income funds. AT&T, the long-distance telephone company, sports a dividend yield of 3.3 percent and earnings are growing at an annual rate of 16 percent. AT&T is expected to have $70 billion in sales by year-end 1993, up from $63 billion in 1991. Exxon, the world's largest oil company, sports a dividend yield of 4.6 percent. Earnings are growing at a 7 percent annual rate, while sales should hit $110 billion by year-end 1993.

The 25 largest growth-and-income portfolio holdings are listed in Table 7.2.

SOME OF THE BEST MUTUAL FUND PERFORMERS

Some of the all-time best performing mutual funds are either growth or growth-and-income funds.

Table 7.2.   Growth-and-Income Holdings

Portfolio			Top 25 Holdings	
Share Change	Amount 000	Stock	Value $000	% Net Assets
	22638	Philip Morris	1772080	1.42
	10857	General Electric	820350	0.99
	7249	Merck	1187970	0.98
	13716	IBM	1236711	0.94
	10196	Bristol-Myers Squibb	885576	0.91
	11766	Exxon	704963	0.85
	10501	FNMA	709476	0.84
	13186	Texaco	808624	0.69
	6000	American Home Products	477432	0.67
	23675	AT & T	923929	0.67
	3247	Johnson & Johnson	355892	0.67
	10049	Mobil	675589	0.67
	6641	Royal Dutch Petroleum	555163	0.65
	26985	GTE	911179	0.62
	5209	Coca-Cola	394602	0.57
	6505	Pfizer	515534	0.57
	5091	Wal-Mart Stores	289327	0.55
	3810	Procter & Gamble	339349	0.51
	8129	K Mart	389253	0.50
	6824	Schering-Plough	428560	0.50
	8069	Emerson Electric	428816	0.48
	15549	JP Morgan	1022653	0.48
	5260	Boeing	251286	0.47
	10971	Pepsico	365250	0.47
	5764	American Cyanamid	373402	0.46

Source: Morningstar Mutual Funds, Chicago. Used with permission.

You can't go wrong with mutual funds that have stood the test of time—those that have performed well over the past 50 years.

One would think such funds would run out of steam. Surprisingly, most of these long-term favorites have kept pace with the market averages, according to CDA/Wiesenberger data. Over the past half century, the S&P 500 Stock index grew at an annual rate of 11.5 percent. Over the past 3 years, ending in May 1992, the S&P 500 grew at an annual rate of 12.7 percent.

Here is a rundown of some of the best-managed mutual funds. All of the funds have outperformed the S&P 500 over the past 50 years, ending in 1990. Over the past 3 years, ending in June 1992, however, most performed as well as the market averages or a little better.

- Investment Company of America (800-421-9900), a growth-and-income fund, grew at an annual rate of 13.09 percent over 50 years. Over the past 3 years, the fund grew at an annual rate of 12.7 percent, the same as the S&P 500.
- Affiliated Fund (800-426-1130), a growth-and-income fund, grew at an annual rate of 12.51 percent over the past 50 years. Over the past 3 years, the fund grew at an annual rate of 9.9 percent.
- Seligman Common Stock Fund (800-221-2450), a growth-and-income fund, grew at an annual rate of 12.42 percent over the past 50 years. Over the past 3 years, the fund grew at an annual rate of 13.7 percent.
- Fidelity Fund (800-522-7279), a growth-and-income fund, grew at an annual rate of 12.41 percent over the past 50 years. Over the past 3 years, the fund grew at a 10.1 percent annual rate.
- Seligman Growth (800-221-2450), a growth fund, grew at an annual rate of 12.41 percent over the past 50 years. Over the past 3 years, the fund grew at an annual rate of 12.3 percent.
- Mass Investors Trust (800-343-2829), a growth fund, grew at an annual rate of 12.01 percent

over the past 50 years. Over the past 3 years, the fund grew at an annual rate of 11.9 percent.

- State Street Investment Fund (617-428-3920), a growth fund, grew at an annual rate of 11.89 percent over the past 50 years. Over the past 3 years, the fund grew at an annual rate of 12.8 percent.
- Putnam Investors (800-225-1581), a growth fund, grew at an annual rate of 11.87 percent over the past 50 years. Over the past 3 years, the fund grew at an annual rate of 12 percent.
- United Income (913-236-1303), an equity income fund, grew at an annual rate of 11.71 percent over the past 50 years. Over the past 3 years, the fund grew at an annual rate of 11.6 percent.
- Safeco Equity Fund (800-426-6730), a growth-and-income fund, grew at an annual rate of 11.68 percent over the past 50 years. Over the past 3 years, the fund grew at an annual rate of 11.4 percent.

CHAPTER 8

Worldwide Mutual Fund Investing

If you want to increase your return and reduce the risk of losing money when the U.S. stock market tumbles, consider keeping part of your investments in global stock and bond funds. These funds invest both here and overseas, so you benefit from worldwide diversification.

Our financial markets are not the only game in town. That's why the money pros look for profitable investments overseas. William Holzer, manager of the Scudder Global Fund, for example, stresses that there are a lot of investment opportunities elsewhere since about two-thirds of the world's securities markets exist outside the United States.

"Over the long run, it's profits that matter," says Holzer. "The profits of a large percentage of the corporations I invest in, regardless of where their headquarters are located, are determined by global supply and demand. That's why it's important to invest around the world."

Economic reports indicate that investors can profit from growing economies overseas. Although Russia and Eastern Europe are in political turmoil, the late Kenneth Oberman, former manager of the

Oppenheimer Global Fund, believed the longer-term outlook is positive. Russia and other states of the former Soviet Union and Eastern European countries are entering the free market. The European business community is uniting into a common economic group this year.

The Pacific Basin and Far East are also hotbeds of growth, according to a recent report published by the G.T. Global Financial Services. Cheap labor and efficient production in the Pacific Basin are resulting in expanding business. In the Far East, Thailand's exports have tripled over the last decade and its stock exchange grew 120 percent in more than one year. Malaysia is also going great guns. Its foreign investment was up 88 percent last year and manufacturing output increased 11 percent over the past 6 years. Singapore's economy grew at a 9 percent annual clip over the past several years. Japan's economy is expected to grow about 3.6 percent this year, despite an economic slowdown and a steep stock market correction.

BENEFITS OF WORLDWIDE DIVERSIFICATION

There is plenty of worldwide potential for investment profits. But does this mean you should buy stocks in Thailand or in Europe?

Not necessarily. The experts say you should invest in a mutual fund that owns securities in several countries. The reason: The world's stock and bond markets don't move in the same direction at the same time. That means that losses here at home would be offset by gains overseas. Over time, analysts say, an investment that owns securities worldwide will be less volatile than an investment that sticks to one country.

"Studies show that you reduce your risk by

investing a portion of your assets overseas," says John Slater, analyst with Kemper Securities and author of *Safe Investing*, published by the New York Institute of Finance in 1991. "You will also increase your returns by investing in foreign stocks and bonds. Many foreign markets have historically out-performed the U.S. markets."

Slater notes that there are three types of *overseas mutual funds* to pick from. The international funds generally invest only in overseas markets and skip the U.S. market. However, some funds—called global funds—may take a stake in the U.S. market. Country-specific funds invest in one country such as Germany or Britain. These are the riskiest type of overseas funds because they are not diversified by country. In contrast, the global funds give you the most diversification because they invest around the world.

overseas mutual funds: funds that invest in stocks or bonds in foreign countries (Global funds invest both here and abroad; international funds invest strictly overseas.)

Although you can invest internationally or globally for profits and safety, financial planners say you should assess your level of risk before di-versifying overseas.

"You have to ask yourself how much you are willing to lose in a given year," says Daniel Todzia, president of Southeast Financial Planning, Inc., in Stuart, Florida. "You have to evaluate your finan-cial needs and zero in on how much risk you are willing to take to achieve your goals."

Once you have a clear picture of your financial situation, you can put part of your investment pie in a global or overseas mutual fund. This move enables you to earn the best return with the least amount of risk. For example, Todzia says that in-vestors willing to assume moderate risk could earn 80 percent of the return on U.S. stocks with 40 percent less risk by keeping an overseas stock fund in their portfolio. This means that if the U.S. stock market dropped 10 percent, a mutual fund portfolio that included an 11 percent stake in a small-company U.S. stock fund, a 24 percent position in a U.S. growth-and-income fund, a 38 percent position in an international fund, and a 27 percent position in a money fund would lose about 6 percent.

Adding a global bond fund to a fixed-income portfolio will also reduce risk and increase yield. For example, when you combine foreign bonds with U.S. bonds, you will earn higher returns with less price volatility when interest rates change here at home because you are diversified worldwide. A mix of 60 percent U.S. bonds and 40 percent foreign bonds has almost 50 percent less price volatility than a 100 percent stake in our bond market.

THE RISKS

There are risks when you invest overseas. In addition to risking losses resulting from an overall decline in a country's stock market prices or bad news about a specific company's financial condition, you face other risks such as *foreign currency risk*. If the dollar gains in value against foreign currencies, the market value of your overseas fund will decline because the stocks are purchased in foreign dollars. Or, a political crisis could lead to a decline in stock prices. Finally, the financial reporting standards about a firm's finances are different in other countries. Analysts don't have the same kind of detailed financial information on foreign companies that they can obtain on U.S. companies.

foreign currency risk: occurs when the market value of an investment changes with the value of the currency used to purchase a security

OUTLOOK FOR OVERSEAS BONDS

Global bond fund managers say that sluggish economic growth throughout the world makes the long-term bonds of several foreign nations attractive.

Judy Pagliuca, manager of the Fidelity Global Bond Fund, which yields 9.54 percent and has grown at an 11.13 percent annual rate over the past 5 years, favors the European bond market because of high rates, low inflation, and sluggish economies. About one-third of her portfolio is invested in money market securities in high-yielding countries such as Spain, Sweden, the United Kingdom, Denmark, Germany, and Finland. Another 46 percent is invested in U.S. investment-grade corporate bonds with average maturities of 6 years. The U.S. bond position adds stability and helps diversify the portfolio.

Global equity fund managers are less sanguine about the overseas stock markets than are the fixed-income portfolio managers. David Testa of the T. Rowe Price International Fund, up 17.5 percent annually over the past 10 years, is cautious about the current outlook because of weak economic recoveries in most major countries and slow growth in Japan and Germany.

Testa observed that the earnings growth has been poor in most major countries, including the United States, Japan, the United Kingdom, and Germany for the past two years. But he expects a modest recovery in corporate earnings overseas as interest rates decline. In addition, he expects a "moderately favorable market environment" in the United States, if corporate earnings improve.

"The European markets appear to have the best prospects in '93 because stocks are undervalued compared to the U.S.," says Testa. "Growth should begin to revive in the U.K. and should accelerate through most of the continent. But the slow German economy will be an exception due to the development in Eastern Europe."

Testa also sees "muted" performance in Japan, but economic growth in other Southeast Asian countries is expected to remain strong. In addition, he predicts that South American markets will continue to perform well.

William Holzer, manager of the Scudder Global Fund, which has grown at an annual average rate of 13.8 percent over the past 10 years, is less optimistic about the European stock markets. He says he's leery of the short-term political situation in Russia and Eastern Europe, so he's reduced his exposure in Europe to 31 percent of the portfolio from 51 percent a year ago.

Holzer says he is also concerned about the high interest rates in Europe and the run-up of stock prices here at home. Germany has to keep rates high to attract the investment capital it needs to reunify the nation, he reasons. Because of that, other European countries that have their currencies tied to the deutsche mark have seen their interest rates move up. So high interest rates, coupled with a recession in Europe, spell double trouble for the equity markets. Although Holzer is not as bearish as some of his colleagues, he is also keeping the portfolio well diversified. Currently, the Scudder Global Fund is 36 percent invested in the United States, 31 percent in Europe, 26 percent in the Far East, including Japan, and the remainder in Canada, Mexico, and South America.

In contrast to the pessimistic global fund managers, Kenneth Oberman, manager of the Oppenheimer Global Fund, up at a 17.4 percent average annual rate over the past 10 years, is a long-term bull on Europe. He thinks that the recapitalization of Eastern Europe will benefit pollution control and heavy industries. He likes firms like Brown Boverie, a large Swiss manufacturer of electrical equipment, and Mannesmann, a German industrial conglomerate.

In the United States, he sees environmental ex-

Table 8.1.   Top-Performing Overseas Funds

5 Years

Net Assets 03/31/92	Name	TR% 5 Yr	Rank All	Obj
1410.9	Templeton Foreign	12.87	55	1
1933.2	EuroPacific Growth	10.67	168	2
109.5	Ivy International	10.08	252	3
38.1	GAM International	8.69	692	4
55.0	Smith Barney International Equity	8.17	853	5
442.8	G.T. International Growth	7.90	918	6
1588.5	T. Rowe Price International Stock	6.95	1082	7
796.5	Trustees' Commingled International	6.48	1138	8
928.3	Scudder International	5.76	1196	9
13.7	Managers International Equity	5.73	1199	10
67.2	Kleinwort Benson International Equity	5.62	1203	11
36.2	IAI International	5.44	1213	12
169.2	Kemper International	5.24	1230	13
58.6	Fidelity Intl. Growth & Income	5.10	1235	14
831.3	Vanguard World International Growth	4.87	1246	15
193.5	Alliance International A	4.41	1259	16
307.5	United International Growth	4.34	1265	17
132.6	International Equity	3.96	1284	18
884.8	Fidelity Overseas	3.84	1288	19
107.7	FT International Equity	3.76	1291	20
	Avg. Annual Return / # of Funds	4.85		28

Source: Morningstar Mutual Fund Performance Report, Chicago. Used with permission.
Note: TR% is the total return percentage over the indicated period. Total returns over 5 years are annualized.

penditures tripling to $175 billion by 1995. That's why he has a stake in Waste Management, whose earnings he expects to see grow at double-digit rates over the next several years.

Table 8.2.   Changes in Major International Markets

For the 12 months ending March 31, 1992

	Return of Unmanaged Index	Local Currency vs. U.S. Dollar	Dollar-Adjusted Return of Unmanaged Index
EUROPE			
Austria (CBSI)	− 14.7%	3.3%	− 11.8%
Belgium (Brussels SE)	− 1.0%	3.9%	2.8%
Denmark (CSEI)	− 5.1%	3.5%	− 1.9%
Finland (Helsinki)	− 28.5%	− 9.5%	− 35.4%
France (CAC 40)	6.9%	3.6%	10.8%
Germany (FAZ)	8.2%	3.9%	12.4%
Greece (General Index)	− 30.1%	− 3.2%	− 32.4%
Ireland (ISEQ Index)	− 7.5%	3.8%	− 4.0%
Italy (B.C.I. General)	− 13.5%	2.9%	− 11.1%
Netherlands (CBS General)	2.3%	4.4%	6.8%
Norway (Oslo Ind.)	− 0.5%	3.9%	3.4%
Portugal (BTA Index)	− 15.0%	6.0%	− 9.8%
Spain (Madrid SE)	− 9.9%	2.3%	− 7.9%
Sweden (Bourse General)	− 8.3%	4.0%	− 4.6%
Switzerland (S.B. Ind.)	11.1%	− 3.6%	7.1%
United Kingdom (FT All-Share)	− 1.8%	− 0.2%	− 2.0%
AUS-ZEAL			
Australia (All Ordinaries)	9.6%	0.1%	9.7%
New Zealand (NA40)	8.9%	− 6.3%	2.0%
FAR EAST			
Hong Kong (Hang Seng)	31.8%	1.4%	33.6%
Indonesia (Jakarta Composite)	− 31.7%	− 3.9%	− 34.4%
Japan (Nikkei)	− 26.2%	6.2%	− 21.6%
Korea (KCSPI)	− 6.6%	− 6.5%	− 12.6%
Malaysia (KLSE Composite)	1.0%	7.7%	8.9%
Philippines (MSE Total Avg)	− 0.4%	11.7%	11.2%
Singapore (OCBC)	− 2.8%	9.0%	6.0%
Taiwan (Weighted Index)	− 6.6%	6.8%	− 0.3%
Thailand (SET Index)	− 5.0%	− 0.3%	− 5.2%
NORTH AMERICA			
Canada (TSE)	− 2.4%	− 2.6%	− 5.0%
United States (S&P)	7.6%	0.0%	7.6%

Source: Morgan Stanley Capital International, Geneva. Used with permission.

HOW TO PICK A FUND

When shopping for an overseas fund, you should check several criteria before you invest. For example:

- As with other funds, check the load, management, and other fees the fund charges.
- Look at the long-term track record. What is the fund's annual rate of return over the last several years? What do the year-by-year returns look like?
- How is the fund diversified? Check the countries and industry breakdown of the portfolio.
- If it's a bond fund, check the yield, average maturity, and total return on the fund.
- Is the fund part of a fund family? If yes, you can then diversify your mutual fund holdings.

Table 8.1 lists the top-performing overseas mutual funds for the past 5 years ending in March 1992. Table 8.2 shows the changes in major international markets for the 12 months ending in March 1992.

CHAPTER 9

Balanced and Income Funds

If you're concerned about risk but still want to keep your hand in the stock market for the long term, consider investing in balanced funds. These are lower-risk mutual funds that have historically lost less money in bear markets than other types of stock funds.

balanced funds: funds that invest in both stocks and bonds, usually with a stock-to-bond ratio of 60:40 (Some funds also diversify among domestic and overseas seucrities.)

Balanced funds typically hold a portfolio that can be as high as 60 percent in bonds, preferred stocks, and cash and only 40 percent in equities. Some balanced funds go as high as 70 percent in stocks and 30 percent in bonds. By investing in a balanced portfolio, you have less exposure to stocks than you would have in a growth fund, so the investment is less risky.

Take 1987, for example, the year the S&P 500 dropped 500 points in one day, October 19. Top-rated balanced funds avoided the full impact of the stock market correction. The Strong Investment Fund, being conservative, had 68 percent invested in cash and only 32 percent in stocks. Massachusetts Financial's Total Return took a middle-of-the-road stance two weeks prior to the October 1987 stock market crash. The fund had 7 percent in cash and notes, 61 percent in stocks, and 32 percent in bonds.

Because of the asset mix, balanced funds emphasize minimum investment risk without sacrificing long-term growth and current income. The funds have beta values of 0.5 percent to 0.6 percent. That means they are less volatile than the stock market. On the upside, they will underperform the market averages, but on the downside they will lose half as much as a growth stock mutual fund. There are several reasons for this. Balanced funds pay higher dividends, so losses are cushioned. In addition, there is a low correlation between stock and bond performance. Although bond and stock prices may both decline, during the longer term the assets tend to move independently of one another. So losses in stocks would, for example, be offset by gains in bonds.

Historically, balanced funds have outperformed the market averages on the downside. They lose money, too, but not as much. For example, from year-end 1968 through year-end 1970, balanced funds lost 4.8 percent while the Dow and S&P 500 declined 11 percent. From year-end 1972 through year-end 1975, balanced funds lost 10.5 percent while the Dow Jones Industrial Average dropped 16.4 percent and the S&P 500 declined 23.6 percent. From year-end 1976 through year-end 1978, balanced funds gained 2.4 percent while the Dow dropped 19.9 percent and the S&P 500 lost 10.6.

In 1987, the same phenomenon held true. Balanced funds gained 2.05 percent. By contrast, aggressive growth funds and growth funds lost 2.7 percent and 2.13 percent, respectively. Ditto for 1984. Balanced funds gained 7.2 percent while aggressive growth funds lost 13.7 percent.

Over the longer term, balanced funds have provided safety-minded investors with solid lower-risk returns than would be possible with a 100 percent stake in the stock market. According to *Morningstar Mutual Funds*, balanced funds grew at a 13 percent annual rate over the past 15 years ending in 1991.

The conservative balanced funds invest in well-seasoned large companies that pay high dividend yields. The average market capitalization of balanced funds at this writing is $6.2 billion. The average dividend yields are about 3 percent to 5 percent.

The largest holdings of balanced funds include such tried-and-true companies as IBM, Philip Morris, General Electric, Bristol-Myers, Squibb, Pfizer, and Johnson & Johnson.

The more aggressive balanced funds will buy smaller stocks in hot industries in the hope of reaping extra profits. For example, the 20th Century Balanced Fund grew at a 16 percent annual rate for 3 years ending in July 1992. The fund picked up big gains in hot growth stocks in the biotechnology, health care, and specialty retailer industries.

On the fixed-income side, the conservative balanced funds invest in money market instruments, U.S. government securities, and investment-grade-rated bonds. By contrast, more aggressive balanced funds will attempt to pick up extra yield by putting money into lower-credit-rated junk bonds that pay yields of 10 percent or more.

Two of the most tried-and-true balanced funds are Fidelity Puritan Fund and Vanguard's Wellington Fund. *Morningstar Mutual Funds* has given both funds top ratings based on return versus risk.

Fidelity Puritan invests in high-dividend-yielding large- and medium-sized stocks as well as bonds. At this writing, the fund has 56 percent in stocks, 36 percent in bonds, and the rest in cash and convertible bonds. Over the past 15 years, the fund has grown at an annual rate of 14.8 percent.

The Wellington Fund will invest up to 60 percent to 70 percent in stocks and the remainder in investment-grade bonds. Like Puritan, the fund likes to invest in higher-dividend-yielding under-valued stocks. Over the past 15 years the fund has grown at an annual rate of 13.8 percent. At this writing, the fund has 57 percent of its assets in stocks, 40 percent in bonds, and the rest in cash.

Table 9.1 lists the leading balanced funds for the 5-year period ending June 1992.

ASSET ALLOCATION FUNDS

Asset allocation mutual funds are another type of balanced fund. The funds invest in stocks, bonds, and cash. They may also invest in overseas stocks and bonds. Some funds invest in precious metals and mining stocks as an inflation hedge.

These funds can be considered core investments for those who want professional management. They allow investors to participate in the growth of the stock market but are less risky than common stock funds.

Asset allocation funds attempt to provide investors the best possible return while taking the least amount of risk. By mixing a portfolio with different types of assets, the fund managers can reduce the volatility of the fund. They avoid larger losses because the funds are hedged. Fund managers who divvy up their portfolios among stocks, bonds, cash, and sometimes precious metals aim to preserve capital while still keeping their hands on some growth stocks.

At year-to-date ending in June 1992, asset allocation funds were down 1 percent compared with a 2 percent decline in the S&P 500. By contrast, aggressive and small-company stock funds lost 8.5 percent and 7.3 percent, respectively.

Over the past 5 years, ending in June 1992, asset allocation funds grew at an annual rate of 9.1 percent. The average diversified equity fund grew at an annual rate of 9.6 percent.

Table 9.1.   Leading Balanced Funds

5 Years

Net Assets 03/31/92	Name	TR% 5 Yr	Rank All	Rank Obj
20.5	Pasadena Balanced Return	18.37	4	1
205.2	State Farm Balanced................	14.55	33	2
358.4	National Income & Growth A....................	11.36	115	3
994.4	Fidelity Balanced......................	11.17	133	4
14.5	Olympic Balanced Income......	10.69	165	5
1386.9	Phoenix Balanced.....................	10.51	188	6
318.0	Pax World	10.07	256	7
429.2	CGM Mutual.............................	10.01	271	8
713.0	American Balanced	9.66	366	9
199.3	Dodge & Cox Balanced	9.63	379	10
1780.2	Vanguard STAR	9.61	383	11
1036.4	Mass. Financial Total Return ..	9.29	479	12
5205.1	Fidelity Puritan...........................	9.27	483	13
824.2	Kemper Investment Part. Total Return...............................	9.22	500	14
552.6	George Putnam Fund of Boston A	9.11	547	15
2000.8	IDS Mutual	9.00	596	16
229.1	Citibank IRA CIT Balanced.......	8.88	633	17
205.6	Eaton Vance Investors.............	8.81	652	18
4118.9	Wellington................................	8.80	654	19
100.0	Sentinel Balanced	8.42	773	20
	Avg. Annual Return / # of Funds...	8.13		44

Source: Morningstar Mutual Fund Performance Report, Chicago. Used with permission.
Note: TR% is the total return percentage over the indicated period. Total returns over 5 years are annualized.

Table 9.2 lists the top-performing asset allocation funds over the past 5 years ending in June 1992.

Table 9.2. Leading Asset Allocation Funds

			Rank	
Net Assets 03/31/92	Name	TR% 5 Yr	All	Obj
22.8	MIMLIC Asset Allocation	11.55	103	1
241.3	Shearson Strategic Investors..	10.37	204	2
26.8	Elfun Diversified......................	10.11	248	3
370.0	Stagecoach Asset Allocation.	10.06	262	4
92.4	Connecticut Mutual Total Return..	9.24	490	5
625.2	Dreyfus Capital Value.............	8.71	685	6
9.0	North American Conserv. Asset Alloc................................	7.91	915	7
330.9	PaineWebber Asset Allocation B..............................	7.78	946	8
274.7	Oppenheimer Asset Allocation...................................	7.68	964	9
29.1	North American Moderate Asset Alloc................................	6.38	1148	10
32.2	Westwood Equity Institutional...............................	6.27	1156	11
128.1	Blanchard Global Growth.....	3.88	1286	12

Source: Morningstar Mutual Fund Performance Report, Chicago. Used with permission.
Note: TR% is the total return percentage over the indicated period. Total returns over 5 years are annualized.

Some asset allocation funds are more aggressive than others. Portfolio managers will shift assets based on their forecasts in an attempt to pick up larger gains in the stock markets. The more conservative funds make smaller asset shifts less often than their aggressive cousins.

Although all asset allocation funds split up the investment pie to reduce risk, they use different strategies. Some funds, such as the Blanchard Strategic Growth Fund, Dreyfus Capital Value, and the Oppenheimer Asset Allocation Fund, will go for the long ball and invest heavily in stocks or bonds worldwide when the fund managers believe economic conditions and price trends are favorable. Others, like the MIMLIC Asset Allocation Fund, Overland Express, Wells Fargo Fund, and the Prudential Bache Flexible Conservative Fund, try to hit singles and keep a conservative mix of assets based on computer models that measure risk-return relationships among groups of assets.

The Permanent Portfolio and the USAA Cornerstone Funds take a similar conservative approach to splitting up the investment pie. These funds have a fixed-percentage range that they can invest in different assets.

BALANCED FUNDS OF FUNDS

Another type of balanced fund is known as the fund of funds. The Vanguard Star Fund and the T. Rowe Price Spectrum Fund, for example, own shares in other funds in the fund family. In other words, you can buy one fund that invests a percentage of its assets in other funds in the group. This way you get diversification and a lower-risk investment.

The Vanguard Star Fund, says Bryan Mattes, spokesperson for the fund group, is designed primarily for retirement savings accounts. The fund invests about 60 percent to 70 percent of its assets in Vanguard's Windsor, Windsor II, and Explorer funds. Thirty percent to 40 percent of assets are invested in the fund group's bond and money funds. Over the past 5 years ending in June 1992, the fund grew at an annual rate of 10.2 percent.

The Spectrum Growth Fund invests in seven of T. Rowe Price's overseas and domestic stock funds. The Spectrum Income Fund invests in seven of T. Rowe Price's bond funds, including U.S., overseas, high-yield, and government funds. Both types of funds are relatively new. At this writing, the Spectrum Growth Fund has gained 9.2 percent for the 12 months ending in June 1992. The Spectrum Income Fund has gained 13.9 percent during the same time frame.

INCOME FUNDS

If you are looking for income first and limited growth second, then the low-risk income common stock funds may be right for you.

Income funds are another type of balanced fund that's tilted toward income and capital preservation. The funds are ideally suited for investors who are living on a fixed income or those looking for an alternative to certificates of deposit (CDs). The funds have typically paid higher yields than the S&P 500 and provided investors with sufficient returns over inflation. For example, over the past 10 years inflation grew at a 3.8 percent annual rate. By contrast, income funds grew at a 13.3 percent annual clip, representing a 9.5 percent return after inflation.

Income funds: funds that invest in high-dividend-paying stocks

This kind of return over the inflation rate makes income funds ideal for systematic withdrawals. A retiree living on a fixed income could take 5 percent out of the fund for income. The portfolio would still grow at 4 percent and keep pace with the rate of inflation, assuring that your investment would hold its purchasing power in years to come.

Income funds typically own more bonds than stocks in their portfolios. For example, at year-end 1991, 60 percent of income funds assets were invested in bonds, 29 percent in stocks, and the rest in cash, preferred stocks, and convertible bonds.

As a result of this type of investment mix, at this writing income funds are sporting dividend yields ranging from 4 percent to as high as 8 percent.

The stocks owned by income funds pay high dividend yields. Typically the funds invest in utility, natural resources, financial services, and nondurable companies that pay out a high percentage of their earnings to shareholders in the form of dividends.

Table 9.3 shows the largest holdings of income mutual funds.

Typically income funds own government securities and investment-grade-rated bonds issued by the most creditworthy corporations based on Standard & Poor's and Moody's bond ratings. A few funds, however, will boost the yield on their portfolio by investing heavily in lower-credit-rated junk bonds.

Income funds have performed well over the past few decades as interest rates have declined, bond prices have risen, and the stock market has soared. Income funds have grown at an average annual rate of 12.4 percent over the past 15 years, 13.3 percent over the past 10 years, and 9.3 percent over the past 3 years.

Income funds are not without risk, however. Because the funds invest in bonds and interest-sensitive stocks like utility companies and natural resources firms, when interest rates rise, income funds may decline in value. Or, if the stock market tumbles, income stocks may be pulled down along with it. As a group, income funds are likely to underperform other types of stock funds in a bull market—that is, over the long term you will not get the capital appreciation from an income fund that you would get from a growth stock fund.

Nevertheless, income funds are less risky than diversified common stock funds. For example, ac-

Table 9.3.   Largest Holdings of Income Funds

Portfolio			Top 25 Holdings	
Share Change	Amount 000	Stock	Value $000	% Net Assets
	2446	Texas Utilities	95286	0.56
	304	AT & T	12203	0.50
	1761	Commonwealth Edison	59944	0.48
	2433	Southern	80180	0.48
	32	Merck	5262	0.47
	1816	Houston Industries	78557	0.42
	1208	FPL Group	42804	0.39
	50	Philip Morris	3924	0.34
	1358	El DuPont de Nemours	64673	0.33
	53	Meditrust	1604	0.33
	1310	Texaco	75325	0.33
	2179	Pacific Gas & Electric	67997	0.32
	1380	American Electric Power	45585	0.31
	880	SCE	39111	0.31
	180	Corning	6098	0.30
	96	Health & Rehabilitation Ppty	1344	0.27
	116	Saint Jude Medical	5551	0.27
	110	General Public Utilities	2840	0.26
	25	Telefonos de Mexico	1228	0.25
	61	Southtrust	1782	0.24
	31	American Health Property	1112	0.23
	44	Boeing	2144	0.23
	580	BP Prudhoe Bay Royalty	16533	0.23
	212	British Telecommunications	7925	0.23
	1811	Entergy	49584	0.23

Source: Morningstar Mutual Funds, Chicago. Used with permission.

cording to CDA/Wiesenberger, over the past 10 years ending in June 1992, income funds have registered an average annual return of 13.7 percent. The high was 17.5 percent and the low was 8.4 percent.

By contrast, growth-and-income funds have registered an annual rate of return of 15.6 percent over the past 10 years ending in June 1992. Although the return on a growth-and-income fund is higher than on an income fund, the range between the high and the low on growth-and-income funds is 20.1 percent and 0 percent.

Frazier Evans, chief economist of the Colonial Funds in Boston, favors income funds for low-risk investors who can't tolerate the volatility of the stock market.

"If the average annual total return in the 1990s is about 9 percent and you can make 5 percent in dividends, you'll be more than halfway there with much less risk than if you invested for capital appreciation," says Evans. "Dividends are upfront payments."

Evans believes that investors should make at least 5 percent in dividends annually over the next decade from income funds. He reasons that the dividends on utility stocks are now averaging over 6.5 percent and energy stocks, from 4.5 percent to 5 percent. Dow Chemical, IBM, and Eastman Kodak, for example, yield over 4 percent. Even better, many of the biggest companies currently have a lot of potential for dividend increases.

There are several well-managed income funds on the market today. According to *Morningstar Mutual Funds*, the Franklin Income Fund, Income Fund of America, USAA Mutual Income, and the Wellesley Income Fund are the best-rated income funds based on return versus risk. The funds carry five-star ratings because their managers get the best returns by taking the least amount of risk compared with other income funds on the market today.

The Wellesley Income Fund is a no-load fund that keeps 60 percent to 70 percent of its assets in fixed-income securities. Over the past 3 years, the fund grew at a 9.6 percent annual rate of return. The fund yields 7 percent and at this writing has 60 percent of its assets invested in investment-grade-rated bonds. Almost 60 percent of the stock portion of the portfolio is invested in utility stocks. The fund's largest holdings include high-dividend-yielding New York Stock Exchange–traded stocks like Exxon, Mobil Oil, Eastman Kodak, Southwestern Bell, Commonwealth Edison, GTE, and NYNEX.

USAA Mutual Income is another high-yielding, no-load income fund. Over the past 3 years, the fund has grown at an annual rate of 12.63 percent. The fund can invest up to 100 percent of its assets in short-term bonds. Normally the fund is heavily weighted toward bonds. At this writing, the fund has 84 percent of its assets in bonds, 21 percent in stocks, and 5 percent in cash. The fund's stockholdings are invested 100 percent in utility stocks such as Texas Utilities, Southern Company, Ohio Edison, and FPL Group. As a result, the fund sports a yield of 7.8 percent.

The Income Fund of America, which carries a 5.75 percent load, is a more aggressive income fund. Over the past 3 years, the fund has grown at an annual rate of 10.9 percent. The fund sports a yield of 6.4 percent and will invest for long-term growth if the portfolio manager sees an opportunity for profits. At this writing, the fund has 38 percent of the portfolio in bonds and 43 percent in stocks. The remainder is invested in cash and convertible bonds. Forty-one percent of the stockholdings are invested in utilities and 30 percent in financial services equities. Largest holdings include IBM, GTE, JC Penney, Commonwealth Edison, and Banker's Trust of New York.

The Franklin Income Fund, a 4 percent–load fund, is more aggressive on the income side of the portfolio than are the other three funds. The fund manager has the flexibility to mix the portfolio to maximize income and to obtain growth. The fund's current yield of 10 percent is due to its large holdings in junk bonds or lower-credit-rated bonds. Forty-three percent of the portfolio is invested in junk bonds, with another 10 percent invested in investment-grade bonds. On the stock side, the fund has invested 74 percent of its assets in utility companies. Over the past 3 years the fund has grown at a 14 percent annual rate. Largest stock-holdings in the fund at this writing include Pacific Gas and Electric, Southern Company, Texas Utilities, Houston Industries, and American Electric Power.

HOW TO PICK SAFE FUNDS

When shopping for a balanced or income fund, check the following:

- Loads, fees, and other mutual fund charges
- Annual compound rates of return over several years and year-by-year performance
- Stock and bond split on balanced funds
- Stock and bond split on income funds
- Average maturity and types of bonds held by the fund
- Industry diversification and types of stocks owned by the fund

CHAPTER 10

Bond Funds

Most people invest in bond funds for safety, liquidity, and yield. They want to know that their principal is secure, they want to be able to access their money quickly if they need it, and they want interest income.

Chapter 3 discusses the risks and rewards of fixed-income investing. To refresh your memory:

1. You face interest rate risk. Bond prices and interest rates move in opposite directions. The longer a bond's maturity, the greater the change in price, up or down, with a change in interest rates.

2. You face credit risk. You could invest in a firm that goes bankrupt. As a result, you may not get all of your principal and interest back.

3. You face opportunity risk. You could lock into a rate only to find rates rising later on.

4. If you invest in foreign bonds, you also incur foreign currency risk.

5. You face reinvestment risk. If you buy a bond and interest rates decline, you have to reinvest your interest income at a lower rate than the rate paid by your bond.

6. In addition, fixed-income investors face purchasing power risk. You get a fixed amount of interest from bond funds. At maturity, you collect your principal. But if inflation has risen over the years, your bond proceeds have less buying power than when you purchased the bond.

A LOOK AT MONEY MARKET MUTUAL FUNDS

money market mutual funds: funds that invest in short-term money market instruments such as Treasury bills

Money market mutual funds are considered a safe investment. The funds invest in short-term money market instruments such as bank certificates of deposit (CDs), commercial paper (corporate IOUs), U.S. Treasury bills (T-bills) and other government securities, Eurodollar CDs (U.S.-dollar-denominated CDs issued by banks overseas), Yankee dollar CDs (CDs issued by foreign banks located here at home), and bankers' acceptances (short-term loans involved in trade).

Money funds are required by law to keep the average maturity of the fund at 90 days or less. This enables the fund to maintain a net asset value of $1. Short maturities also reduce credit risk. The shorter the time span of the loan, the less time there is for something to go wrong with a company. A lender faces less risk of default when a contract to lend a company money runs for 30 days rather than 30 years.

Although money funds invest for the short term, the fund managers have the flexibility to increase their yields. When interest rates rise, managers shorten the average maturity of the portfolio. That way they have money to invest in higher-yielding securities when the existing investments mature. And when rates decline, fund managers lengthen the average maturity of the portfolio to lock into higher money market rates.

There are also several types of money funds on the market. Every mutual fund family carries one or a stable of money funds for its investors. Among these various types are:

• *Government-only money funds.* These funds invest only in T-bills and U.S. government securities. These funds are considered less risky than other funds because the investments are backed by the full faith and credit of the U.S. government or have the moral backing of Uncle Sam.

• *General purpose money funds.* These funds invest in both government, corporate, and bank securities. The funds pay higher yields than Treasury money funds because there is greater credit risk in lending money to a bank or corporation compared with lending money to the U.S. Treasury.

• *Tax-free money funds.* These funds invest in short-term municipal (muni) notes. Income from the funds is free from federal taxes. Single state muni bond funds are exempt from both state and federal income taxes.

• *Overseas money funds.* These funds invest in foreign-denominated money market investments. At this writing, the overseas funds are paying higher yields than U.S. money funds. However, there's greater risk that the market value of the investment could decline if the dollar strengthens against foreign currencies. Because of the foreign currency component, overseas money fund or short-term bond fund portfolios fluctuate in value.

GOVERNMENT BOND FUNDS

If you want to avoid credit risk, buy funds that invest in Treasury securities and government agency obligations.

There are several types of government bond funds to pick from. There are short-, intermediate- and long-term funds that invest in Treasury bonds and/or U.S. government agency obligations. The short-term funds have average maturities ranging from about 2 to 5 years. The intermediate funds invest in bonds that mature in 5 to 10 years. The long-term funds invest in bonds that mature in 10 years or more.

You can also invest in zero-coupon government bond funds. These funds invest in zero-coupon bonds, which are bonds that sell at a bid discount to face value. You collect both principal and interest when the bonds mature.

Several government bond funds invest 100 percent of assets in U.S. Treasury securities. These funds include the Benham Target Maturities 2015, a zero-coupon Treasury bond fund; Benham Treasury Note Fund; ISI Total Return U.S. Treasury; Midwest Income Intermediate Term Government Fund; and the Vanguard Fixed Income Long Term U.S. Treasury Bond Portfolio.

There are also government bond funds that invest in mortgage-backed securities issued by the Government National Mortgage Association (GNMA), Federal National Mortgage Association (FNMA), the Federal Housing Authority (FHA), and the Department of Veterans Affairs (VA). Hybrid funds will invest in Treasury securities, mortgage bonds, and other U.S. government agency issues such as the Small Business Administration or the Student Loan Marketing Association.

GNMA, FNMA, FHA, and VA agencies raise money in the bond market to make home mortgages. The principal and interest paid every month by the homeowner are passed through to the bondholders. For that reason, the bonds are called passthrough certificates. In addition, the bonds are considered to be free of credit risk because the government agencies back the bonds against default.

Mortgage bond funds pay higher yields than Treasury bond funds because they have higher risks. When interest rates fall, homeowners refinance their high-rate mortgages at lower rates. As a result, bondholders get back principal and interest earlier than expected. The more homeowners pay off their old mortgages, the less you will earn on your mortgage bond or bond funds.

Over the past 10 years, mortgage bond funds have outperformed Treasury bond funds. Mortgage funds grew at a 12.28 percent annual rate compared with a 9.22 percent annual rate for Treasury funds.

Top-rated mortgage bond funds, according to *Morningstar Mutual Funds*, include Federated Income Trust, Franklin U.S. Government, Vanguard Fixed Income GNMA, Kemper U.S. Government, Lord Abbott U.S. Government, Prudential GNMA B, and Lexington GNMA.

ADJUSTABLE-RATE MORTGAGE FUNDS

Last year a new kind of mortgage bond fund became available to investors. Adjustable-rate mortgage (ARM) funds invest in mortgage bonds tied to adjustable-rate mortgages. These funds earn about 3 percent more than CDs and money funds. An ARM fund's price volatility is about the same as that of a 1-year Treasury bill. This means that if a 1-year bond is yielding 5.5 percent and interest rates rise 1 percent, the total return on your investment, which includes interest income plus price appreciation or loss, is 4.35 percent. In other words, you have lost about 1 percent on your money.

ARM funds are considered a low-risk alternative to money funds. However, financial planners like Robert Klein, columnist for *Financial Services Week* in New York, believes that ARM funds have a lot more price volatility than money funds not only because of changes in interest rates but also because of the scarce supply of ARM bonds in the marketplace. Supply and demand determine the price of any security. When there is a big demand to buy a bond and the supply is short, the price of the bond will rise. Conversely, if investors sell and the supply increases, the price of the bonds will fall. Therein lies the problem with ARM funds—you get higher than money market rates but increased price volatility.

CORPORATE BOND FUNDS

Corporate bonds earn higher yields than government securities. The reason: Investors are compensated for taking risks by receiving higher yields. In addition to being exposed to interest rate risk, you face credit risk when you invest in corporate bonds. You can control some of the interest rate risk by investing in a corporate bond fund with a shorter average maturity. But a corporation that falls on hard financial times may have a problem repaying principal and interest. If the company goes bankrupt, bondholders may have to sell for 10 to 20 cents on the dollar to realize anything on their investment.

There are several different kinds of bond funds to pick from, depending on your tolerance for risk. High-grade corporate bond funds invest in bonds rated triple-B (BBB) to triple-A (AAA) by Standard & Poor's and Moody's Investors Services. The bond in the portfolio are considered investment grade, which means you are investing in the most creditworthy issuers. High-grade corporate bond funds also may hold a small percentage of their investments in U.S. government securities. By law, however, a high-grade fund must hold at least 65 percent of its assets in investment-grade-rated bonds.

Check the prospectus of the corporate bond fund before you invest. Some funds will boost yields by investing in the lower-tier investment-grade-rated bonds that carry single-A (A) or triple-B (BBB) ratings. The lower-yielding investment-grade-rated funds will generally hold more upper-tier investment-grade-rated bonds. For example, at this writing, the AARP High Quality Bond Fund sports a yield of 6.5 percent because 80 percent of the portfolio is invested in triple-A-rated corporate bonds and U.S. government bonds. By contrast, the Paine Webber Investment Grade Income Fund, which yields 7.9 percent, has half the portfolio invested in single-A, triple-B, and a smattering of single-B-rated bonds.

High-yield bond funds are a different ball game. These funds invest in what are called junk bonds, or bonds issued by less creditworthy corporations. Junk bonds carry ratings that range from single-B to triple-C to no rating at all. Because of the high credit risk, junk bond funds earn high yields. At this writing, you could earn a 10 percent yield if you invested in one of these funds.

Junk or high-yield bond funds are a high-risk gambit. As long as the economy is healthy, there is less risk that bond issuers will default on their obligations. However, during a recession, the number of defaults increases. In 1990, for example, junk bond funds lost 10 percent in value. The next year, the funds gained 35 percent as the market rebounded. To stock market investors, that's not much of a loss to take for a subsequent gain. To someone who is living on a fixed income, however, junk bond funds can be a wild ride.

Convertible bonds are yet another type of fixed-income mutual fund. These give you the best of both worlds—income from a bond and a play on the company's underlying stock. Convertible bonds are complex instruments. In a nutshell, when you invest in a convertible bond fund, you own bonds that can be converted into a company's stock. For that reason, the bond's price is determined not only by the goings-on in the bond market but also by how well the company's stock is performing.

The *United Mutual Fund Selector (UMF)*, a Massachusetts-based mutual fund newsletter, calls convertible bond funds "a mutual fund for all seasons."

If you are uncertain about the outlook for stocks or bonds, convertible bond funds may be a good investment.

"As the stock market goes up, these hybrid mutuals allow investors to share in some of the price rise," says a recent *UMF* report. "By contrast, should the market correct, the yield advantage of convertibles cushions some of the downside price movement compared with pure equity funds. If there is little movement either way in the market, convertibles typically offer the advantage of higher yields. This is a meaningful benefit in today's low interest rate environment."

If you are shopping for a convertible bond fund, Jack Walsh, editor of *UMF*, recommends the following funds: Fidelity Convertible Securities Fund, up 13.6 percent over the past 5 years ending in 1991; American Capital Harbor Fund, up an average of 10.5 percent annually over the same time frame; and Vanguard Convertible Fund, up an average of 8.1 percent annually over the same period.

MUNICIPAL BONDS FOR TAX-FREE INCOME

If you are in the 28, 31, 36, or 39.6 percent tax bracket, you will benefit from investing in municipal bond funds. These funds invest in bonds issued by state and local governments and government agencies. The bonds are issued to raise money for public projects and services like road building, water and waste treatment facilities, airports, and toll roads.

Municipal bonds come in many shapes and sizes, just like Treasury and corporate bond funds. There are tax-free money funds, short-term muni bond funds, long-term muni bond funds, and high-yield muni funds.

Municipal bonds invest in several different types of tax-free securities. In any muni bond fund you will find the following holdings:

municipal bonds: funds that invest in tax-free bonds issued by state and local governments

• *General obligation bonds.* These bonds are backed by a state or city's ability to tax its citizens. A populated state that has high employment and a state income tax would have a strong base to back up its bonds and repay principal and interest to its bondholders.

• *Revenue bonds.* These are tax-free bonds backed by income received from toll roads, hospitals, water-usage fees, utilities, and publicly financed businesses.

• *Special tax bonds.* These bonds are backed by a specific tax, like a property or gasoline tax, to raise funds for special projects.

• *Municipal notes.* These are short-term bonds or IOUs that mature in 30 days. The bonds are issued in expectation of future revenues, taxes, and the sale of bonds.

• *Project notes.* These are short-term bonds issued by local housing authorities and urban renewal agencies. The notes are backed by the U.S. government.

• *Insured municipal bonds.* Bonds that carry high credit ratings may also carry muni bond insurance. Insurance companies like MBIA, Inc., AMBAC Indemnity Corp., and Financial Guarantee

Insurance Corp. (FIGIC) will insure timely principal and interest payments in the event an entity defaults. The bonds pay lower yields than comparable uninsured bonds because of the cost of obtaining insurance.

Municipal bond interest income is free from federal income taxes. If you invest in muni bonds issued by your state of residence, the bonds are also free of state and local taxes. By owning them you get double or triple tax-free income. There are numerous bond funds on the market that are state specific.

Municipal bonds carry credit ratings by Standard & Poor's and Moody's. Triple-A rated bonds are considered the most creditworthy. Bonds rated single A to triple A are considered investment-grade-rated bonds. Standard & Poor's says that A-rated issuers are considered to have "a strong capacity to pay interest and repay principal although they are somewhat more susceptible to adverse changes in circumstances and economic conditions than debts in higher-rated categories."

Triple-B rated issuers are also considered highly creditworthy by both rating agencies. However, these issuers could run into financial hot water during poor economic times and may have problems paying bondholders.

Bonds rated double B, single B, triple C and double C and C are considered speculative. D-rated issuers are already in default.

TAX-FREE RETURNS

If you are in a high tax bracket, the tax-free income from muni bonds is nice to have. However, you will have to pay Uncle Sam and your state a capital gains tax on any profits generated from the sale of your bonds or bond funds.

Table 10.1. Tax-Exempt Yields and Their Taxable Equivalents

Tax Exempt Yield	Tax Equivalent Yield	
	Federal Tax Rate	
	36%	39.6%
4.0%	6.25%	6.61%
4.5	7.03	7.44
5.0	7.81	8.26
6.0	9.38	9.92
6.5	10.16	10.74
7.0	10.94	11.57
7.5	11.72	12.40
8.0	12.50	13.22
8.5	13.28	14.05

Tax-free bonds are quoted in after-tax rates. So before you invest, you need to determine the taxable equivalent yield on the muni bonds. At today's rates, you can earn 5 percent tax free in a well-managed municipal bond fund. That translates into taxable equivalent yields of 6.9 percent, 7.25 percent, 7.81 percent, and 8.26 percent if you are in the 28, 31, 36, or 39.6 percent tax brackets, respectively.

That's not bad considering that comparable Treasury securities are paying pretax yields of just 6 percent. You are earning an equivalent of 1 percent more from a muni bond fund.

You will get a bigger break if you invest in a double tax-free fund. On average, for example, someone in the 36-percent tax bracket who also pays state income taxes would earn a taxable equivalent yield of 8.7 percent at today's rates.

Calculating your taxable equivalent yield is

pretty easy. Divide the tax-free rate by 1 minus your tax bracket. For example: 5 percent divided by $(1 - .28 = .72)$ equals 6.9 percent. Table 10.1 shows you the federal taxable equivalent yields on muni bond funds.

HOW TO PICK TAXABLE OR TAX-FREE BOND FUNDS

Whether you are shopping for a Treasury fund, corporate bond fund, or municipal bond fund, you need to be aware of several important factors. John Bogle, chairman of the Vanguard Group of Investment Companies in Valley Forge, Pennsylvania, suggests the following criteria to use when evaluating a fixed-income fund:

• Assess your tolerance for risk. Longer-term bonds show greater price fluctuation in response to changes in interest rates than do short-term bonds (see Table 10.2). If you want higher yields from long-term bond funds, you have to accept that if interest rates rise, the fund's net asset value (NAV) will decline a lot more than will the NAV of a money fund or short-term bond fund. If interest rates were to rise by 1 percent, a 6.5 percent long-

Table 10.2. Percentage Change in Value of Bond If Interest Rates Move

U.S. Government Security	Up 1%	Down 1%
Money Fund	0%	0%
3-month T-Bill	− 0.24	+ 0.24
1-yr T-Bill	− 0.93	+ 0.94
5-yr T-Note	− 3.83	+ 4.01
10-yr T-Note	− 6.17	+ 6.72
30-yr T-bond	− 9.40	+ 11.23

term bond would lose almost 12 percent in value. By contrast, a 1-year bond would lose 1 percent.

• Consider both the yield and total return on the bond fund. Bond funds have two yields. The Securities and Exchange Commission's mandated yield represents the rate based on interest income from the bonds. The stated yield on the bond will reflect both interest income and capital gains.

Total return is also an important consideration when shopping for a bond fund. Total return represents both income and capital appreciation of the fund. Say a fund yields 6 percent and the fund's net asset value increases 4 percent; your total return is 10 percent. Total return reveals the portfolio manager's ability to navigate safely in the financial markets. You could buy a fund with a whopping 10 percent yield, but a year later your total return is just 3 percent. You collected 10 percent in interest income but you lost money on your principal.

Tables 10.3 through 10.8 list top-performing bond funds for a 5-year period ending June 30, 1992.

• Consider the credit ratings of the bonds held in the portfolio. Lower-credit-rated bonds pay higher yields, but there is a greater risk that the issuers could default or have problems paying back principal and interest.

• Consider a bond's prepayment risk. Mortgage bonds face prepayment risk. When interest rates decline, homeowners pay off their existing home loans and refinance at a lower rate. If you own a bond fund with a large stake in mortgage bonds, you face a greater chance that the investments will be prepaid.

• Consider foreign currency risk. Funds that own overseas bonds face currency risk. If the dollar gains against the value of foreign currency, the market value of bonds denominated in that currency will decline. Funds often hedge against cur-

Table 10.3. Leading Municipal Bond—National Funds

5 Years

Net Assets 03/31/92	Name	TR% 5 Yr	Rank All	Obj
63.3	UST Master Tax-Exempt Long-Term	11.68	94	1
888.5	United Municipal Bond	10.51	187	2
752.8	General Municipal Bond	10.37	205	3
1356.3	Vanguard Municipal High-Yield	10.31	215	4
216.0	Alliance Muni. Income National	10.20	232	5
379.5	Premier Municipal Bond	10.08	253	6
251.8	Financial Tax-Free Income Shares	10.08	255	7
883.7	Vanguard Municipal Long-Term	10.07	257	8
318.3	Nuveen Insured Municipal Bond	10.02	268	9
1612.4	Putnam Tax-Exempt Income	9.99	277	10
93.0	Eaton Vance Municipal Bond	9.98	280	11
427.6	SAFECO Municipal Bond	9.95	291	12
396.9	SteinRoe High-Yield Municipals	9.93	294	13
472.9	Lord Abbett Tax-Free Income National	9.91	298	14
1740.7	Vanguard Municipal Insured Long-Term	9.90	301	15
260.7	Smith Barney Muni Bond National	9.89	303	16
162.9	Scudder High-Yield Tax-Free	9.86	310	17
68.9	PaineWebber Municipal High-Income A	9.84	317	18
779.7	Scudder Managed Municipal Bonds	9.83	319	19
24.3	First Trust Tax-Free Bond Income	9.81	324	20
	Avg. Annual Return / # of Funds	8.65		135

Source: Morningstar Mutual Fund Performance Report, Chicago. Used with permission.
Note: TR% is the total return percentage over the indicated period. Total returns over 5 years are annualized.

rency risk, but the hedges are short term and imperfect.

• Look at your tax situation. If you are in the 28, 31, 36, and 39.5 percent tax bracket, you may earn higher taxable equivalent yields from municipal bond funds.

Table 10.4. Leading Government Bond—Treasury Funds

5 Years

Net Assets 03/31/92	Name	TR% 5 Yr	Rank All	Obj
158.4	Benham Target Maturities 2005	13.36	45	1
125.2	Benham Target Maturities 2000	12.88	54	2
54.1	Benham Target Maturities 2010	12.01	82	3
86.6	Benham Target Maturities 1995	11.64	96	4
28.5	Scudder Zero Coupon 2000	10.58	180	5
165.5	Benham Target Maturities 2015	10.49	189	6
202.0	Dreyfus 100% U.S. Treasury Long-Term	10.17	236	7
818.4	Vanguard Fixed-Inc. Long-Term U.S.	10.11	247	8
12.0	Scudder Zero Coupon 1995	9.81	323	9
26.2	Rushmore U.S. Govt. Long-Term	9.65	368	10
193.2	Dreyfus 100% U.S. Treasury Interm	9.51	409	11
31.3	Wright Government Obligations	9.48	422	12
16.5	Rushmore U.S. Govt. Intermed.-Term	9.32	469	13
32.1	Principal Pres. Government	9.31	475	14
727.6	Federated Interm. Govt. Institutional	9.28	481	15
301.5	Benham Treasury Note	8.80	655	16
35.1	Columbia U.S. Government Securities	8.41	774	17
46.5	Midwest Income Intermed.-Term Govt.	8.34	803	18
1168.3	Federated Short-Interm. Govt. Instit.	8.32	809	19
	Avg. Annual Return / # of Funds	10.08		

Source: Morningstar Mutual Fund Performance Report, Chicago. Used with permission.

• Check the fund's loads, fees, and expense ratios. The more fees and commissions you pay, the less you have in your pocket. Bond funds with a high expense ratio eat into your returns. The lower the bond fund's expense ratio the better the deal.

Table 10.5. Leading Corporate Bond— General Funds

5 Years

Net Assets 03/31/92	Name	TR% 5 Yr	Rank All	Obj
62.6	FPA New Income	11.47	106	1
76.3	Dreyfus Strategic Income	11.33	117	2
99.0	Mackenzie Fixed-Income	11.21	130	3
1796.4	PIMCO Total Return	11.20	131	4
99.7	UST Master Managed Income	11.06	141	5
71.0	Wright Current Income	10.68	167	6
36.6	Managers Fixed-Income Securities	10.63	174	7
38.6	Calvert Income	10.53	184	8
538.5	Putnam Income	10.48	191	9
46.5	SEI Instit. Mgd. Bond A	10.36	207	10
143.0	Elfun Income	10.35	209	11
452.9	Mass. Financial Bond	10.29	217	12
829.3	Lutheran Brotherhood Income	10.21	230	13
899.9	PIMCO Low Duration	10.21	231	14
39.8	Asset Management Interm. Mtg. Secs.	10.14	241	15
3018.8	Bond Fund of America	10.10	249	16
907.7	Fidelity Investment Grade Bond	10.10	250	17
45.8	Sentinel Bond	10.00	272	18
1255.1	John Hancock Sovereign Bond	9.95	290	19
117.9	TNE Bond Income	9.94	292	20
	Avg. Annual Return / # of Funds	9.16		52

Source: Morningstar Mutual Fund Performance Report, Chicago. Used with permission.

Table 10.6.   Leading Corporate Bond—Quality Funds

5 Years

Net Assets 03/31/92	Name	TR% 5 Yr	Rank All	Obj
2070.4	Vanguard Fixed-Inc. Invstmt. Grade	11.14	136	1
400.5	Shearson Investment Grade Bond	10.57	182	2
221.5	Columbia Fixed-Income Securities	10.49	190	3
116.7	Babson Bond L	10.31	214	4
4.0	Wasatch Income	10.25	223	5
396.2	Scudder Income	10.03	264	6
330.1	Merrill Lynch Corp. High-Quality A	9.99	279	7
841.2	Vanguard Bond Market	9.97	286	8
446.9	Dreyfus A Bonds Plus	9.93	293	9
228.7	SteinRoe Intermediate Bond	9.92	297	10
65.4	Alliance Bond Monthly Income	9.87	305	11
214.9	PaineWebber Investment Grade Income A	9.87	308	12
107.6	IAI Bond	9.83	318	13
1297.3	T. Rowe Price New Income	9.80	328	14
1435.6	IDS Selective	9.80	329	15
119.4	Twentieth Century Long-Term Bond	9.80	330	16
66.1	Nationwide Bond	9.58	389	17
96.0	Pioneer Bond	9.51	408	18
2028.4	Vanguard Fixed-Inc. Short-Term Corp	9.49	417	19
269.0	AARP High-Quality Bond	9.45	431	20
	Avg. Annual Return / # of Funds	9.22		42

Source: *Morningstar Mutual Fund Performance Report*, Chicago.
Used with permission.

Table 10.7.   Leading Government Bond— Mortgage Funds

5 Years

Net Assets 03/31/92	Name	TR% 5 Yr	Rank All	Obj
171.2	Managers Intermediate Mortgage Secs..	11.33	119	1
120.0	Premier GNMA	11.25	128	2
5428.6	Vanguard Fixed-Income GNMA	11.13	137	3
55.8	Investors Preference Fund for Income	10.91	147	4
720.4	Benham GNMA Income	10.88	149	5
18.3	MIMLIC Mortgage Securities Income	10.87	150	6
1370.9	Federated GNMA Institutional Shares	10.86	152	7
130.8	Princor Government Securities Income	10.84	153	8
129.3	SEI Cash + Plus GNMA A	10.83	154	9
35.2	Smith Barney Monthly Payment Govt	10.83	155	10
396.2	Smith Barney U.S. Government Secs	10.79	159	11
82.1	Asset Management Mortgage Secs. Perf	10.68	166	12
153.1	Franklin Tax-Advantaged U.S. Govt	10.41	200	13
537.8	Alliance Mortgage Securities Income A..	10.30	216	14
3349.6	Van Kampen Merritt U.S. Government	10.28	218	15
156.2	First Trust U.S. Government	10.25	222	16
58.2	Connecticut Mutual Government Secs	10.22	225	17
2536.4	Lord Abbett U.S. Government Secs	10.22	226	18
1278.5	Federated Income Institutional Shares	10.07	258	19
423.7	Fidelity Mortgage Securities	10.03	265	20
	Avg. Annual Return / # of Funds	9.79		

Source: Morningstar Mutual Fund Performance Report, Chicago. Used with permission.

**Table 10.8.   Leading Government Bond—
General Funds**

5 Years

Net Assets 03/31/92	Name	TR% 5 Yr	Rank All	Obj
52.9	Strong Government Securities	11.91	87	1
2789.5	General Electric S&S Long-Term Int	10.57	183	2
12.8	State Bond U.S. Government Securities	10.36	208	3
379.6	Value Line U.S. Government Securities	10.12	244	4
2123.1	Merrill Lynch Federal Securities A	10.11	245	5
33.0	Sit "New Beginning" U.S. Govt. Secs	10.07	261	6
10.1	Franklin PA Investors U.S. Govt	10.02	269	7
222.4	WPG Government Securities	10.01	270	8
146.5	Composite U.S. Government Securities	9.97	285	9
479.4	Fortis U.S. Government Securities	9.92	296	10
347.2	John Hancock Government Spectrum	9.91	300	11
1383.1	Fund for U.S. Government Securities	9.85	312	12
180.6	Freedom Government Income B	9.85	315	13
66.0	Mutual of Omaha America	9.84	316	14
4020.2	AARP GNMA & U.S. Treasury	9.74	345	15
297.6	First Investors Government	9.71	350	16
491.2	Fidelity Government Securities	9.71	351	17
28.5	Heartland U.S. Government	9.71	352	18
3679.5	American Capital Government Secs. A.	9.69	357	19
376.7	Federated ARMs Institutional Shares	9.67	362	20
	Avg. Annual Return / # of Funds	8.89		

Source: Morningstar Mutual Fund Performance Report, Chicago.
Used with permission.

CHAPTER **11**

Sector Funds

sector funds:
funds that invest in
specific industries
such as utilities,
chemicals, or
technology

Most sector funds are considered speculative investments. *Sector funds* invest in a specific industry such as high technology, forest products, chemicals, and biotechnology.

When you invest in a sector fund, you are betting on an industry. You don't have the diversification you get from an equity fund that invests in a number of different industries and holds a large number of stocks.

Utility stocks are an exception to the rule. Utility stock funds invest in a large number of utility companies. The industry is considered recession resistant. It's a cash cow business: Everyone turns on the lights, no matter what shape the economy is in. Later on in the chapter is a discussion about the risk and rewards of investing in utility stocks.

Several fund groups have a stable of sector funds that includes a money fund. Most are low- or no-load funds. Fidelity Investments select portfolios have 36 sector funds to pick from. Financial Funds has the Financial Strategic portfolios. Vanguard offers the Vanguard Specialized portfolios. Both have 10 funds in their portfolios. You will pay a low-load and a redemption fee when you invest in the Fidelity select portfolios. Vanguard charges a redemption fee, while Financial portfolios are load free.

Numerous other fund groups may have one or two industry-specific funds. For example, the G.T. Fund Group has a Global Health Care Fund. Oppenheimer has a Global Biotechnology Fund in its stable. Colonial Investments has a Natural Resources Fund. Putnam has an Information Science Fund.

Unlike diversified equity funds, sector funds are volatile performers. You may be in for a wild roller coaster ride when you invest in a sector fund. For example, Fidelity Select Technology gained 52.5 percent in 1983. The next year it lost 16.9 percent. In 1985 the fund gained back 7.5 percent. Then it lost 29 percent over the next 3 years.

THE BUSINESS CYCLE TELLS YOU WHEN TO INVEST

If you want to invest in sector funds, you have to look at the performance trends of a sector fund and keep a close watch on the business cycle. Some industries do better than others during periods of economic growth or high inflation and rising interest rates.

Recent advisory reports say the market could go above the current high, but it will be an extremely volatile ride. The higher the stock market rises, the greater the chance of a correction.

Even though you may buy and hold or make periodic payments into your mutual funds, timing is still an important factor. Who wants to enter the market with fresh money and end up 10 percent in the hole right from the start?

There is no perfect timing mechanism. Buying opportunities arise during different phases of the business cycle. The business cycle is usually considered to be about a 4-year period during which the economy moves from recession to economic growth before again subsiding into recession. During that time, certain industries benefit from the ensuing business conditions and show greater profits.

Several buying opportunities occur during a four-phase business and investment cycle.

1. The recession phase is characterized by high unemployment and poor business performance. It's the result of high inflation and high interest rates. During this time, the safest performers are short-term bonds, money funds, and Treasury bills. Mutual funds that invest in safe industries like tobacco, foods, drugs, hospital supplies, soaps and, in some cases, banks should also show less loss on the downside.

2. During a corrective phase, interest rates and inflation start to decline. Falling interest rates boost bond and share prices of financial services, utility, and blue-chip stocks.

3. During the improvement stage, health care, leisure, and technology should be hot sectors.

4. During the inflation phase, inflation hedges like energy, natural resources, and gold funds will perform well. As inflation rises, the economy will move into stagnation during which time interest rates and inflation are both high. It is a period that kicks off a recession.

GOLD AND PRECIOUS METALS FUNDS

precious metals mutual funds: funds that own gold and mining stocks; may also invest in related metals and mining operations

If you want a hedge against inflation, consider investing in *precious metals mutual funds*. These funds perform well when inflation heats up. Unfortunately, they fall behind when inflation is low, as it is today.

Mutual funds that invest in gold and other precious metals mining stocks lag behind other types of mutual funds during periods of low inflation. For example, precious metals funds have grown at an annual rate of − 4 percent over the past 3 years ending in June 1992, this at a time when the annual inflation rate grew 3.5 percent.

During the same time period, the average diversified equity fund gained 8.94 percent annually and the average fixed-income fund grew at a 9.7 percent annual rate.

That doesn't bode well for precious metals and gold funds. But look what happens when inflation heats up. From year-end 1978 through year-end 1988, inflation grew at an annual rate of 6 percent. Gold funds grew at an annual rate of 16.3 percent during that time frame. By contrast, the average fixed-income fund gained 10.7 percent and the stock market grew at an annual rate of 16.3 percent, according to Lipper Analytical Services.

Precious metals mutual funds are volatile investments. During periods of high inflation you can earn fat returns. In 1979, for example, the average precious metals fund gained 164 percent. But in other years, you would have lost your shirt.

Financial planners say there are two ways to invest in precious metals. As a rule of thumb, they suggest always keeping 5 percent of your assets in the shiny metal just in case inflation rears its ugly head. Others say that if you want to speculate, you should consider subscribing to an investment advisory service that follows gold bullion and mining stock price trends. Newsletters like these will tell you when to buy and sell precious metals.

Table 11.1 lists top-performing precious metal mutual funds for the 10-year period ending June 30, 1992.

UTILITY STOCK MUTUAL FUNDS BEST BET FOR RECESSION

Yields of 5 percent plus and double-digit performance gains over the past several years make utility stock

Table 11.1.   Top-Performing Precious Metal Mutual Funds

		10 Years		
Net Assets 03/31/92	Name	TR% 10 Yr	Rank All	Obj
254.4	Franklin Gold..	11.85	421	1
89.2	Lexington Goldfund...............................	9.31	481	2
512.1	Van Eck International Investors..........	9.21	483	3
137.6	Fidelity Select Precious Metals/Min...	7.79	492	4
25.1	Bull & Bear Gold Investors..................	3.91	503	5
212.6	United Services Gold Shares...............	1.41	508	6
17.9	Lexington Strategic Investments.........	−6.83	511	7
	Avg. Annual Return / # of Funds.....	5.24		

Source: Morningstar Mutual Funds Performance Reports, Chicago. Used with permission.
Note: TR% is the total return percentage over the indicated period. Total returns over 10 years are annualized.

mutual funds a low-risk way for safety-conscious people to invest for the long term.

The several utility stock funds tracked by Morningstar, Inc. in Chicago have competitive yields of up to 8 percent but differ in their investment objectives. Some funds, such as Fidelity Select Electric Utilities, look to hit home runs for growth, while others, such as ABT Utility and Franklin Utility, provide investors with steady income at lower risk than the S&P 500. Still other funds, such as Prudential Bache Utilities, have focused on total return by combining both growth and income stocks in the portfolio.

Some funds salt their portfolios with telephone and natural gas stocks. Earnings in both industries are on the rise. The telephone industry is benefiting from new products, technology, and cost cutting. And higher crude oil prices in the 1990s and environmental concerns about coal-fired electric energy producers could lead to more natural gas usage. That, combined with depressed drilling for gas in relation to increased demand, could increase earnings.

For most investors, however, utility stocks are considered a defensive investment that provides people with a steady stream of income. They perform better than other stocks during recessions. Because utilities have a monopoly to sell electricity and gas in specific territories and operate without competition, they are considered an excellent source of dividend income. In addition, utility stocks are traditionally preferred investments during economic recessions because of utility companies' steady demand and cash flow. Utilities are highly regulated, however, by state public utility commissions. Each state regulates rates, construction, and financial plans.

Because of monopoly and regulation, utility stocks exhibit price stability compared with industrial companies. As a result, utility stocks are considered interest-rate sensitive and usually trade at a premium to Treasury bonds. When interest rates rise, utility stock prices drop. Conversely, when rates decline, utility stock prices appreciate.

Ernest Liu, a highly regarded public utility analyst with Goldman Sachs, believes this industry tends to outperform the broad market months before an economic recession. Investors who believe that interest rates are at a peak should consider adding utilities to their portfolios.

For example, Liu noted that since 1945, when interest rates rise, electric utilities underperformed the market. Conversely, when rates decline, utilities outperformed the market. In addition, utilities generally outperform the market during the first two-thirds to three-quarters of a recessionary period. However, when the economy begins to recover, utility stocks begin to lag behind the broad market.

Although utility stocks appear to be recession-proof investments, Alan Berro, utility stock analyst for Fidelity Research & Management in Boston, stresses that the industry faces some major hurdles that make the criteria for stock selection very important. There could be an electricity capacity shortage looming on the horizon. As a result, utilities may have to build new plants and seek rate increases from utility commissions. Expected brownouts this year could prompt rate commissions to permit firms to raise their rates. However, if rates rise too high, Berro believes that large corporate users would start generating their own electricity at a lower cost. This would affect the profitability of utility companies. In addition, new construction would result in increased debt levels.

Berro adds that profits in coal-fired midwestern utility companies could come under pressure if tough new environmental laws are enacted. The installation of antipollution equipment will increase costs. However, he says, there are growth opportunities in turnaround nuclear utility stocks like Public Service of New Hampshire and Long Island Lighting. Some of the strongest and lowest-cost utilities with modest yields are firms like Duke Power, Carolina Power, Consolidated Edison, and Dominion Resources.

Not all utility stock funds are alike. So shop around if you want to invest in a professionally managed portfolio—some funds take more risk than others.

Most utility stock funds invest at least 65 to 80 percent of assets in utility stocks. They may also diversify into gas and telephone companies. The mix, however, can change. Utility funds that seek growth may invest heavily in risky turnaround situations like General Public Utilities or Consumers Power. Other funds that want safety and income will invest more of the portfolio in high-quality utility companies like Commonwealth Edison, Duke Power, and Carolina Power.

Funds that seek higher income invest more heavily in medium-grade utility companies such as Green Mountain Power and Kansas City Power and Light.

PART 3

HOW TO MANAGE
YOUR MUTUAL FUNDS

CHAPTER 12

How to Diversify Your Mutual Fund Investments

What kind of investor are you? Do you like to take risks and invest in aggressive growth or small-company stock funds? Or do you prefer the safety of U.S. government bond funds because there is no risk of default?

You learned in Chapter 4 what kind of investment risks you are comfortable taking. In this chapter, you will read about what type of investments you should own based on your level of risk.

HOW TO DETERMINE YOUR TOLERANCE FOR RISK

The risks you are willing to take depend on a number of factors:

- The economic climate today and what is expected in the future
- Your income and family size
- Your changing financial situation
- Your stage in life

Morton Silverman, managing director at Piper Jaffray & Hopewood, a Minneapolis-based brokerage firm, says, "They [investors] have to make a number of assets work for them over the long term."

Every investor is different, with different financial goals and tolerances for risk. For that reason, Silverman stresses that investors have to practice asset allocation or diversification of the investment portfolio based on their tolerance for risk for a couple of important reasons:

1. Asset allocation serves to reduce the risk of losing money by splitting up your investments among different types of assets. That way losses in stocks are offset by gains in bonds or cash or overseas securities. For example, in 1987, the year of the big stock market crash, aggressive stock funds lost 3 percent but international stock funds gained almost 10 percent. Your stock losses would also have been offset by a 2 percent gain in high-quality bond funds.

2. To make asset allocation work, however, you have to assess your level of risk and define your financial objectives. Based on your age, family size, financial condition, and goals, you have to find the best mix of assets that will maximize your returns.

"Just as there is no one suit of clothes that fits everyone, such is also the case for investment portfolios," says Silverman. "As each of us goes through life, our needs, objectives and tax situations and cash flow requirements change. And as we accumulate wealth, our risk orientation may also change."

Before setting up your investment portfolio, the experts say, you have to take your financial temperature. You have to understand the risks and rewards of owning stocks and bonds. You have to assess how much risk you are willing to take—how much you are willing to see the market value of your portfolio decline in any given year. In addition, you have to evaluate your financial goals before you invest.

Financial data show that investors face a dilemma. If they invest only in stocks, they run the risk of seeing a substantial drop in the market value of their investments in any given year. But if they have the stomach to tolerate losses, they will see their common stock investments grow over the long term. Conversely, if they play it safe and invest in Treasury bills (T-bills) or bonds, their returns will barely keep pace with inflation.

For example, according to Ibbotson & Associates, a Chicago-based analytical firm, the riskiest investments have registered the greatest growth over the long term, although they show the greatest chance for losing money over the short term. For example, small-company stocks have grown at an annual rate of 12 percent over the past 6 decades. But small-company stocks show the greatest volatility. They exhibit a performance margin of error of 35 percent in any given year. That means you run about a 68 percent chance of losing 23 percent or gaining 47 percent in any year; but if you buy and hold stocks over the long term, you will average a return of 12 percent.

Blue-chip stocks have grown at an average annual rate of 10 percent over the past 6 decades. But stockholders have also faced big short-term risks. The margin of error on stocks that make up the S&P 500 is 21 percent. So in any given year, you could expect to lose 11 percent or make 31 percent.

International stocks are also risky. Over the past 30 years, overseas stocks have grown at an annual rate of 13 percent. That looks great, but there's a 20 percent margin of error in the returns from year to year. So you could expect to lose 7 percent or make 33 percent in any given year about 60 percent of the time.

Bonds are less risky than stocks. Over the past six decades, bonds have grown at an annual rate of 4.6 percent. Furthermore, bonds have a margin of error in performance of only 5 percent. So in any given year, you run the risk of losing less than 1 percent or of making 10 percent.

T-bills and other liquid assets are the least risky investments. Liquid assets have grown at an annual rate of about 4 percent over the past 60 years. That's low, but so is the margin of error for losses. You run about a 68 percent chance of making between 1 percent and 7 percent if you own T-bills over the long term.

Table 12.1 gives a historical perspective on market trends over the past 50 years for various types of investment portfolios.

HOW TO ZERO IN ON YOUR FINANCIAL OBJECTIVES

The next step after determining your risk profile is to plan your financial objectives. Ray Linder of LIN-VE$T, located in Great Falls, Virginia, recommends that investors answer three simple questions:

1. Where are you now? Investors need to analyze their current financial situation.
2. Where are you going? Investors should list specific financial goals (i.e., retirement, college expenses, debt repayment, etc.) and determine in how many years money will be needed to fund those goals.
3. How will you get there? Investors must compare the goals in step 2 with their present situation in step 1 and determine what changes need

Table 12.1. Market Trends: Annual Rates of Return

For the Following Periods Ending 12/31/90	Common Stocks	Long-term Govt. Bonds	Long-term Corporate Bonds	Intermediate-term Govt. Bonds	U.S. Treasury Bills	Consumer Price Index
1 Year	−3.2%	6.2%	6.8%	9.7%	7.8%	6.1%
3 Years	14.1	11.2	11.2	9.7	7.5	5.1
5 Years	13.1	10.8	10.4	9.3	6.8	4.1
10 Years	13.9	13.7	14.1	12.5	8.5	4.5
20 Years	11.2	8.7	9.0	9.1	7.7	6.3
30 Years	10.2	6.2	6.8	7.3	6.5	5.1
40 Years	11.6	4.9	5.5	6.1	5.4	4.3
50 Years	12.0	4.5	4.9	5.2	4.4	4.8
Since 12/31/25	10.1	4.5	5.2	5.0	3.7	3.1
After Adjustment for Inflation	6.7	1.4	2.0	1.8	0.5	—

Source: Ibbotson, Roger G., and Rex A. Sinquefield, *Stocks, Bonds, Bills, and Inflation* (SBBI), 1982, updated in *Stocks, Bonds, Bills and Inflation 1991 Yearbook™*, Ibbotson Associates, Inc., Chicago. *All rights reserved.* Used with permission.
Common Stocks (S&P 500)—Standard and Poor's Composite Index, an unmanaged weighted index of the stock performance of 500 industrial, transportation, utility, and financial companies.
Long-term Government Bonds—Measured using a one-bond portfolio constructed each year containing a bond with approximately a 20-year maturity and a reasonably current coupon.
Long-term Corporate Bonds—For the period 1969–1990, represented by the Salomon Brothers Long-term, High-Grade Corporate Bond Index; for the period 1946–1968, the Salomon Brothers Index was backdated using Salomon Brothers monthly yield data and a methodology similar to that used by Salomon Brothers for 1969–1990; for the period 1925–1945, the Standard and Poor's monthly High-Grade Corporate Composite yield data were used, assuming a 4 percent coupon and a 20-year maturity.
Intermediate-term Government Bonds—Measured by a one-bond portfolio constructed each year containing a bond with approximately a 5-year maturity.
U.S. Treasury Bills—Measured by rolling over each month a one-bill portfolio containing, at the beginning of each month, the bill having the shortest maturity not less than 1 month.
Inflation—Measured by the Consumer Price Index for all Urban Consumers (CPI-U), not seasonally adjusted.

to be made to achieve their goals. This is the essence of establishing an investment portfolio.

It will be difficult to achieve any long-term financial goals without a complete understanding of where you are today. You must know conclusively where you are now before you can even consider making plans for the future. There are two traditional financial summaries that will provide you with the information you need to begin planning your financial future:

- Statement of net worth
- Statement of income and expense

A statement of net worth is a snapshot of your present financial condition. It summarizes every financial decision that you've ever made. Basically, this statement lists each asset owned and each liability owed. Subtract liabilities from assets and you have your net worth. The objective is to have your net worth growing at a rate consistent with your future objectives. To begin your analysis, complete the form shown in Figure 12.1.

The statement of net worth contains three critical pieces of information:

- Liquid assets
- Productive assets
- Propensity to borrow

Liquid assets are those assets that can be converted to cash without any penalty or loss of principal. Most advisors recommend that individuals hold liquid assets worth 3 to 6 months of living expenses (see Figure 12.2). However, investors should hold an amount that makes them feel comfortable. From an investment perspective, substantial

ASSETS	LIABILITIES

ASSETS

LIQUID (Nonretirement accounts)
- Checking account _____
- Savings account _____
- Money Market _____
- CDs _____
- Stocks _____
- Bonds _____
- Mutual funds _____
- Life insurance (cash value)
- Other _____

NONLIQUID

Retirement accounts
- IRAs _____
- 401K _____
- Annuities _____
- Other _____

Real estate (resale value)
- Primary residence _____
- Vacation property _____
- Investment property _____

Personal assets (resale value)
- Car _____
- Collectibles _____
- Jewelry _____
- Furniture _____
- Clothing _____
- Other _____

TOTAL ASSETS _____

NET WORTH _____

PRODUCTIVE ASSETS _____

PROPENSITY TO BORROW _____%
(Liabilities divided by assets)

EXPECTED RATE OF RETURN ON PRODUCTIVE ASSETS _____%

LIABILITIES

HOUSING LOANS
- Primary residence mortgage _____
- Second mortgage _____
- Vacation home mortgage _____
- Investment property loan _____

INSTALLMENT LOANS
- Bank loans _____
- Car loans _____
- Student loans _____

CREDIT CARDS _____

OTHER LOANS _____

TOTAL DEBTS _____

LIQUID ASSETS _____
(Assets minus liabilities)

INTEREST RATE ON INSTALLMENT LOANS _____%

Figure 12.1. Statement of net worth "balance sheet."

INCOME (after-tax)	**EXPENSES**
Salary _____	1. Housing
Rental income_____	Mortgage/rent _____
Interest income_____	Maintenance _____
Dividend income _____	2. Food_____
Other income _____	3. Auto
	Loan _____
	Maintenance _____
	4. Utilities _____
	5. Insurance _____
	6. Loans
	Major _____
	Installment _____
	Credit card_____
	Other _____
	7. Entertainment _____
	8. Clothing _____
	9. Medical _____
	10. Miscellaneous _____

NET MONTHLY INCOME _____   **NET MONTHLY EXPENSE** _____

NET MONTHLY SURPLUS _____
(Income minus Expense)

Figure 12.2.   Statement of income and expense "budget."

liquid assets allow the flexibility to take advantage of investment opportunities as they arise.

Productive assets are those assets that have potential to generate income or appreciation. They are the sum of your liquid, nonliquid, and real estate assets and could possibly include some collectibles such as artwork or coins. Productive assets are the key to investment planning. Investors need to ensure that their productive assets are doing two things.

First, your productive assets must match your financial objectives. If you desire growth, then growth-oriented investments such as stocks and long-term bond mutual funds must make up a high proportion of productive assets. Too many investors have excess funds tied up in low-yielding investments like money market funds and CDs. However, these types of fixed-income investments, as well as bonds and dividend-paying equity mutual funds, would be appropriate productive assets for investors desiring income and stability of principal.

Second, your productive assets must be growing faster than your liabilities. If this is not the case, your net worth will actually decline and you will be losing rather than gaining wealth. Credit card debt and high-interest bank loans are the worst liabilities to have because they are often used to buy nonproductive assets that will not contribute to long-term growth in net worth, and because very few investment portfolios can be constructed to earn a rate of return higher than the typical rate of interest on credit cards and other consumer loans. To increase net worth and reach long-term financial objectives, liabilities should be taken on only to finance productive assets—for instance, real estate—and at an interest rate lower than the expected rate of return on your productive assets. If your net worth analysis shows substantial high-cost debt, your best investment decision is to eliminate that debt before making other investments.

A final, useful exercise is to determine your propensity-to-borrow ratio, which is calculated by dividing assets by liabilities. This ratio will show you how likely you are to borrow to accumulate assets. For instance, a propensity to borrow of .65 means that 65 percent of your assets were accumulated by borrowing rather than by paying cash. All things being equal, it is better to have a low propensity-to-borrow ratio because this indicates minimal interest-bearing liabilities and faster growth in net worth. That being the case, it should be an investment-planning objective to reduce your propensity to borrow. This can be accomplished by reducing high-cost debt and by accumulating productive assets.

The second valuable financial summary is a statement of income and expense. This is simply your monthly expenses subtracted from your monthly income. This statement will help you determine the surplus funds you have available for investment purposes.

Careful scrutiny of your expenses will often uncover unnecessary uses of funds that could be used for investing. In investing, little things can mean a lot. Because of the compounding earning power of money, even small amounts of surplus cash can grow to a substantial amount. An investment of an extra $100 per month can become $100,000 in 20 years in a portfolio set up to earn just under 11 percent per year.

The two summary statements will show you where you are now. The next step in portfolio planning is to assess where you desire to go. This is simply a matter of listing your specific financial objectives—retirement, education expenses, housing, and so on. Estimating how much money you will need to fund your goals is obviously crucial to good planning. However, a critical aspect of your "wish" list is an estimate of how soon you will need money for these objectives. How much time you have until you need the money will determine how much risk you can afford to take in investing for these goals. This risk will guide you to the appropriate type of portfolio you should construct.

If your financial goals are less than 1 year away, they are immediate and your portfolio should have virtually no risk, even if you are a higher-risk personality. You need to be absolutely certain about how much money you will have to fund your goals, and you have no time to recover from any loss of principal. Therefore, stability of principal, rather than growth of principal, should be your only portfolio consideration.

If your financial goals are 1 to 5 years away, they are short term. Your portfolio should have low to moderate risk, depending upon your personality. While some level of certainty is needed, with up to 5 years to fund your goals, there is time to recover from investment losses as long as they are not too large. While stability of principal is still a primary concern, growth can be an important secondary consideration. A short-term portfolio should be weighted toward bond and money market funds and low-risk equity funds. The level of equity funds in your portfolio will depend on time and your risk profile.

If your financial goals are more than 5 years away, they are long term. Your portfolio should have as much risk as your personality will allow. Because your goals are more than 5 years away, appreciation of principal is usually the method by which you will achieve your objectives. You should generally weight your portfolio more heavily to equity mutual funds for a greater rate of return. For holding periods of greater than 5 years, most of the volatility and uncertainty associated with the stock market are minimized. Since 1940, the stock market has not lost money in any 5-year period, and stocks have outperformed bonds nearly 80 percent of the time. For longer investment periods, the advantages of the equity market are even more dramatic. For 30-year holding periods since 1929, stocks have outperformed bonds 95 percent of the time while providing investors with five times the return. For long-term investors, the message is clear: Take as much risk as your personality will allow.

HOW TO SPLIT UP THE INVESTMENT PIE

Now that you know your tolerance for risk and your financial objectives, here are some suggested ways to diversify your investment portfolio. There are no hard-and-fast rules on how you should split up your investment pie. Most experts say you should invest in small-company stock funds for maximum growth, growth-and-income funds for stability, and international stock funds for diversification because overseas stocks don't perform in tandem with U.S. stocks. Your fixed-income component should include a money market and/or a short-term bond fund. Short-term bond funds yield about 85 percent of long-term bond funds but have half the price volatility when interest rates rise. High-tax-bracket investors should consider investing in tax-free municipal bond funds.

Using your stage of life as the main criterion, here is how you should split up your mutual fund investment pie, according to leading mutual fund investment advisers.

• *Fancy free and future oriented.*   Wealth builders are people who are willing to assume greater risks in return for long-term growth. Preservation of capital isn't as important as profits. Income isn't an important consideration.

Sheldon Jacobs, publisher of the *No Load Investor*, a newsletter based in Irvington-on-Hudson, New York, says this group of investors should keep the majority of their money in common stocks. Holding on to their investments for the long term will reduce risk because stocks have grown at rates of 10 percent to 12 percent annually.

Another way to cut volatility is to invest in different types of stock funds. Currently, Jacobs is advising investors to keep 35 percent in small-company stock funds for growth; 15 percent in international funds both for growth and to help diversify the portfolio against declines; and the remaining 60 percent in growth-and-income funds for stability. Growth-and-income funds invest in seasoned companies that pay dividends. The dividend income serves as a cushion against losses when the stock market declines.

"There is no hard-and-fast rule about how much you should invest in stocks," says Jacobs. "Everyone is different. There is no set formula for allocating assets. You should tailor your investments to your own situation."

Another recommended mix based on CDA Technologies' asset allocation data base is 13 percent invested in small-company stock funds, 27 percent in growth-and-income funds, 43 percent in international stock funds, and 17 percent in money funds and short-term bond funds. With this kind of mix, you can expect to earn between 23 percent and −1 percent about 68 percent of the time. If the financial markets do well, you have a fifty-fifty chance of earning 11 percent.

• *Family responsibilities* Families need growth, but they can't afford to take too much risk. They need to save for retirement and their children's future college education.

Jonathan Pond, president of Financial Planning Information, Inc., in Watertown, Massachusetts, says the biggest mistake young families make is either chasing after hot stock market mutual funds or keeping too much money in bonds and CDs.

"They either want to get rich quick and chase after top-performing hot stock funds, or they are too conservative and keep everything in federally insured bank accounts," says Pond, who is also the former editor of the *Wiesenberger Mutual Fund Report*. "But I like to tell investors to invest in high-quality, well-managed stock funds. You get professional management and growth."

Pond suggests that young families invest a fixed amount each month (dollar cost averaging) in well-managed common stock funds—funds with consistent long-term track records. He recommends keeping at least 50 percent in stock funds. Families should have at least 3 months' income in cash. The remainder of their portfolio could be invested in short-term bond funds. The funds yield around 8 percent and have less price volatility than long-term bonds when interest rates rise.

CDA Technologies' recommended mix includes 9 percent in small-company stock funds, 19 percent in growth-and-income funds, 32 percent in international stock funds, and 40 percent in money funds and short-term bond funds. With this kind of mix, you can expect to earn between 18 percent and 0 percent about 68 percent of the time. You run a fifty-fifty chance of making 9 percent over the next year.

• *Approaching retirement.* Preretirees want to preserve their capital the closer they get to retirement. However, at this stage in their lives they still need growth because most have life expectancies of at least 20 years or more.

Silverman says the biggest mistake preretirees make is to try to time the markets—move into bonds and out of stocks when it looks like interest rates are on the rise, then move back into stocks to catch a bull market.

"It's difficult to make the shift and time the markets," says Silverman. "It's better to diversify and have a number of assets working for you at all times. You can make 5 to 10 percent changes in your portfolio by rebalancing your mix of assets."

Silverman recommends a diverse portfolio made up of 35 percent growth stocks, 15 percent overseas equities, 5 percent inflation hedges, 10 percent cash, and 35 percent bonds of different maturities.

CDA Technologies' recommended mix includes 6 percent in small-company stock funds, 11 percent in growth-and-income funds, 21 percent in international stock funds, and 62 percent in money funds or short-term bond funds. With this type of mix, you can expect to earn between 14 percent and 2 percent about 68 percent of the time. Over the next 12 months, you have a fifty-fifty chance of earning 8 percent.

• *Senior citizens.* Retirees want income and preservation of capital at this stage of life. Dannial Todzia, president of Southeast Financial Planning in Stuart, Florida, says senior citizens make the mistake of putting too much in bonds and CDs.

"Health care inflation is much higher than the general rate of inflation," says Todzia. "They can't put all their money in CDs and bonds. They lose purchasing power. They have to own stocks for growth."

As a rule, Todzia recommends that retirees keep about 25 percent in bond funds, 25 percent in money funds, and the rest in safe common stock funds for growth. He favors growth-and-income funds, utility stock funds, and high-dividend-yielding stock funds. Adding stock to the fixed-income mix gives retirees some capital appreciation plus a 5 percent dividend income.

Another recommended mix based on CDA Technologies' data is 18 percent in growth-and-income funds, 12 percent in utility stock or income funds, and 70 percent in short-term or intermediate-term bond funds and money funds. With this kind of mix, you can expect to earn between 2 percent and 14 percent. Over the next 12 months you have a fifty-fifty chance of earning 8 percent.

CHAPTER 13

Dollar Cost Averaging and Related Strategies

I f you are the type of investor who looks for simple ways to manage your money, here are several
tried-and-true strategies that you can use with your
mutual fund investments. All you need is an hour
once or twice a year to manage your money like a
pro.

DOLLAR COST AVERAGING

Dollar cost averaging (DCA) is one of the oldest investment concepts in use today. It's a long-term
savings program based on constant buying. Say,
for example, you invest $100 a month into a mutual
fund. By doing this, you purchase more shares in
bear markets when stock prices are on the decline.
As a result, when the market rebounds, the relationship between average cost and market price
favors the investor. The idea is to invest a fixed
dollar amount every month for a long term of at
least 10 to 20 years. That way, you profit from the
long-term growth in the stock market.

If you had used dollar cost averaging to invest
in the Vanguard Index 500 fund, a stock fund that
tracks the performance of the S&P 500, over the

**dollar cost
averaging:**
making regular
investments in a
fund so that over
time, the average
cost of your
investment will be
more than the
current market price
when you sell

past 15 years, ending in June 1992, you would have made a good investment. If you had invested $100 a month, your money would have grown to $63,000, representing a 13.7 percent annual rate of return. Your average cost per share as a result of DCA would have been $22.47, while the current market price at the end of June 1992 was $38.58.

Although DCA may be one of the safest ways to play the stock market, there are pitfalls. Sheldon Jacobs, publisher of the *Handbook for No-Load Investors* and the *No Load Investor* newsletter, published in Irvington-on-Hudson, New York, says there are no guarantees that the average cost will be less than the market value when you redeem your shares. Those who have a sizable lump sum should consider using some type of reliable market timing indicators to get into stocks near the bottom of the market. An upfront investment will show bigger profits during a bull market.

"I don't know if dollar cost averaging makes sense, if someone has $200,000, for example, to invest," said Jacobs. "They [investors] are just playing with themselves, if they divide up the money over 24 months and invest in an equity fund. They are better off doing market timing."

Jacobs says DCA has other shortcomings. First, because bull markets last longer than bear markets, investors may not be able to buy enough shares at a lower cost during the down phase to make it as profitable as lump-sum investment that rides up a bull market. This can happen in a V-shaped stock market cycle that sees a rapid rebound in prices such as occurred in the October 1987 stock market tumble and ensuing rebound.

Second, it takes about 5 years for investors to accumulate enough money in a DCA program to reap substantial profits. So, over the short term, the performance of dollar cost average will lag.

VALUE AVERAGING

There are ways to juice up DCA to boost returns. Several easy-to-use systems incorporate systematic investing with buy-and-sell rules to enhance performance.

In his book *Value Averaging*, Harvard University Business School professor Michael Edleson discusses an aggressive adaptation of DCA.[1]

Dr. Edleson says *value averaging* is similar to dollar cost averaging except that the investor makes the value of the portfolio increase by a fixed amount every month rather than by investing a fixed dollar amount as in dollar cost averaging.

value averaging: a variation of dollar cost averaging that calls for increasing dollar contributions

For example, if you want the value of your investments to increase $100 a month, your actual purchase may range from zero to $100, depending on how much your existing stock or equity mutual fund has increased. You would sell shares when prices rise and the value of the portfolio increases more than $100. That way you take excess profits out of your investment. If share profits drop, however, you have to kick in extra money.

The following hypothetical investment program demonstrates how value averaging works. Say you want the value of your investment to increase $100 a month. In the first month, you invest $100. Your objective is to have holdings worth $200 at the end of the second month. Say the market value of your initial investment went up to $115 by the end of month two. All you have to kick in is $85.

In month three, the market value of your holdings increases to a whopping $250. Your investment that month is $50. But, say, in the next month your investment is worth $425. You then take out

[1] Reprinted from *Value Averaging* by permission of International Publishing Corp., 625 N. Michigan Ave., Chicago, IL 60611.

the excess profits of $25 and sock it away in a money fund.

But what happens if the market value of your investment drops?

Edleson says you have to make up the difference. At the end of month five, your investment should be worth $500. But, say there was a stock market correction and the value of your investment dropped to $375. You then have to kick in another $125 to bring the value back up to $500.

"Value averaging is a more profitable way to invest compared to dollar cost averaging," says Edleson. "Financial studies show that the stock market tends to overreact in the short run, but generally can be counted on to correct itself in the longer run. You win more than you lose, if you stay invested in stocks. That's why value averaging guides you to take advantage of high prices by selling or getting in at low prices by buying before the market moves to another level."

When you use a value-averaging formula, you always take profits when prices are high and buy when prices drop. Edleson says you should adjust your portfolio from one to four times a year for best results. Over time that can lead to solid investment returns. For example, his studies show that value averaging outperformed dollar cost averaging over the past 6 decades from 1926 through 1989. If you adjusted your portfolio quarterly using value averaging, your investment grew at an annual rate of 12.76 percent compared with an annual growth of 11.42 percent using dollar cost averaging. If you adjusted your portfolio once a year, you would have earned 12.54 percent annually with value averaging compared with 11.41 percent with dollar cost averaging.

Over the short term, investors can get some whopping returns with value averaging if they happen to start their investment program after a severe stock market correction. For example, Edleson notes that investors who started using his system right after the stock market crash of October 1987 have registered 20 percent or more annually. Over time, however, returns will drift back to more historical averages of about 12 percent, he points out.

Edleson also stresses that value averaging isn't the secret to stock market success. The big disadvantage of the system, compared with dollar cost averaging, is that it is harder to use and could increase your transaction costs if you don't monitor your investment.

VALUE RATIO INVESTING

Walter Roulea, publisher of *Growth Fund Guide* in Rapid City, South Dakota, has developed a savvy way to make mutual fund switching decisions. He recommends that as the stock market goes higher, investors salt more into conservative equity mutual funds or cash, then wait out the declines and reinvest in stocks when the market again looks overvalued.

There is no surefire way to time the markets. However, Roulea's strategy, called *value ratio investing*, is a disciplined way to make investment decisions. You invest based on the price-to-dividend ratio (PD) on the S&P 500 stock market index. PD is calculated by dividing the dividend yield on the index into the number one. For example, if the stock market yields 4 percent, the PD is 25 (or 1 divided by 0.04). This tells you that you must invest $25 to get $1 worth of dividends.

Historically, Roulea says, the market is overvalued when you must invest $30 to $34 for every $1 of dividends. When a $20 investment returns a $1 dividend, however, the stock market is undervalued. Great buying opportunities exist when the PD is below 20 or when stocks yield 5 percent or more.

Roulea's strategy is an easy one. You always

value ratio investing: an investment tactic whereby money is invested in aggressive stock funds when the stock market is considered undervalued and in conservative funds when the market is overvalued

stay fully invested and split the portfolio between conservative and aggressive equity funds. You can also use a money fund as a conservative investment. When the price-to-dividend ratio is rising, you put more of your money in conservative growth-and-income funds until you are 100 percent invested in safer mutual funds by the time the PD hits 34. As the PD declines, you put more of your money into aggressive growth funds. When the PD goes below 20, you maintain a 100 percent position in aggressive stock funds.

Below is an exact breakdown using Roulea's strategy. For a fully invested stock portfolio, the breakdown is as follows:

- If the PD is 34, you invest 100 percent in conservative stock funds.
- If the PD drops to between 30 and 33.99, you invest 87.5 percent in conservative mutual funds and 12.5 in aggressive stock funds.
- If the PD ranges between 23 and 29.99, you invest 67.5 percent in conservative funds and 37.5 percent in aggressive funds.
- If the PD is between 20 and 23.99, you invest 37.5 percent in conservative funds and 62.5 percent in aggressive funds.
- If the PD is below 20, you invest 100 percent in aggressive funds.

For a stock and cash portfolio, the breakdown is as follows:

- If the PD is 34, you invest 50 percent in money funds and 50 percent in conservative funds.
- If the PD is between 32 and 33.99, you invest 15 percent in money funds, 75 percent in conservative funds, and 10 percent in aggressive funds.

- If the PD is between 30 and 31.99, you invest 10 percent in money funds, 55 percent in conservative funds, and 35 in aggressive funds.
- If the PD ranges from 23 to 29.99, you invest in a mix of 50 percent conservative funds and 50 percent aggressive funds.
- If the PD ranges from 20 to 22.99, you invest 37.5 percent in conservative funds and 62.5 percent in aggressive funds.
- If the PD is below 19.99, you invest 100 percent in aggressive funds.

Roulea notes that his value ratio tactic is a low-risk way to earn mutual fund profits. The portfolio that moves between conservative and aggressive stock funds grew at an annual rate of 14.2 percent over the past 10 years and 13.7 over the past 5 years ending in 1990.

During the same time period, the stock and cash portfolio grew at an annual rate of 15.5 percent and 16.8 percent over the past 10 and 5 years, respectively.

CONSTANT INVESTMENT PLANS

Constant Dollar Investing

Constant dollar investing is another easy-to-use strategy that is one step above dollar cost averaging.

"I like this type of investing," says Dr. Avner Arbel, finance professor at Cornell University. "You are always taking profits and putting the money in a safe place."

Under the constant dollar plan, the dollar value of your aggressive investments remains constant after passing through a predetermined time period. Excess cash is parked in a bond or money fund. Then you switch between the fixed-income and

constant dollar investing: a method of investing whereby a portfolio is rebalanced after a specified period of time to a fixed dollar amount

stock funds to keep a constant dollar amount invested in the stock fund.

Here's how the constant dollar strategy would work using an aggressive growth stock and a bond or money fund: You've decided to keep a constant dollar amount of $10,000 in your aggressive portfolio. Once a year you adjust the portfolio. If the portfolio's value is above $10,000, you take the profits and put them in a money or bond fund. If the value is below $10,000, you take money out of the money or bond fund to bring the stock portfolio back to $10,000.

You can get more sophisticated if, for example, you are willing to accept a 20 percent gain or loss in your stock portfolio every 6 months. After 6 months, if the value of your stock fund has grown to $12,000, you would take out $2,000 and move it into your bond or money fund. Conversely, if the value of your stock fund has dropped to $8,000 after six months, you would switch $2,000 out of bonds and into stocks to maintain the constant dollar value of $10,000. You use the bond or money fund as a parking place—the only reason to change its value is to move money in and out of stocks.

Over the past 15 years ending in June 1992, if you had adjusted your portfolio once a year between the S&P 500 and a money fund, your $10,000 investment would have grown to $49,540, representing an 11.26 percent annual return.

constant ratio investing: a method of investing whereby a fixed percentage of the investment is maintained between stocks and bonds (e.g., 50 percent stocks and 50 percent bonds)

Constant Ratio Investing

Constant ratio investing is another way to buy more shares when prices decline. By maintaining a constant ratio of stocks to bonds or cash over a period of time, you are rebalancing your portfolio by taking profits on the upside and dollar cost averaging on the downside.

Say you kept 50 percent of your $10,000 investment in a stock fund and 50 percent in a bond fund. That's a ratio of 1. Every year you would rebalance to a ratio of 1, or the fifty-fifty split. Over the same time frame of 15 years ending in June 1992, this investment would have grown at an annual rate of 11.78 percent, and your $10,000 investment would be worth $53,145.

REBALANCING AN ALLOCATED PORTFOLIO

The rebalancing strategy goes one step further than the constant ratio tactic. When you rebalance, you maintain the same constant percentage mix in your diversified portfolio. The size and allocation of the percentage portions can be tailored to your specific situation. To cut your risk in the stock and bond markets, you could divide your portfolio into fifths. You could put 20 percent, for example, in U.S. government bond funds, 20 percent in international stock funds, 20 percent in growth-and-income funds, 20 percent in an aggressive stock fund, and 20 percent in a precious metals fund (as an inflation hedge) or in a money fund (as a safety valve).

With this kind of mix, you diversify your holdings so that gains in one type of mutual fund will offset losses in other types of funds. If once a year you had rebalanced the mix using a gold fund instead of a money fund, your money would have grown at an annual rate of 12.72 percent over the past 15 years ending June 1992 compared with a 14.5 percent return on the S&P 500. You earned 93 percent of the return from the stock market but took about one-third less risk than you would have had you been 100 percent invested in the U.S. stock market.

Let's see how the timing would work with a

mix that includes a money fund. In 1981—a bad year for stocks because interest rates were at double-digit levels—the Vanguard Index 500 lost 5.2 percent, the U.S. Gold Fund dropped 27.9 percent, and the Scudder International Fund lost 2.6 percent. Only the money fund, which paid 17.3 percent interest, survived the interest rate debacle. Your $10,000 investment would be worth $9,766 at the end of the year because your portfolio lost 2.34 percent.

But that's more than 50 percent less than you would have lost had you been 100 percent invested in stocks. Although you were down to $9,766 at year-end 1981, you were in a strong position to catch the great 7-year bull market that started in 1982. Stocks gained 21.3 percent and money funds yielded 12.8 percent; at the same time, precious metals rebounded to a 72.5 percent return. As a result, your total portfolio grew 30.37 percent to $12,732.

The 20 percent rebalancing tactic works well to reduce risk. That percentage breakdown may not be ideal for everyone. A couple approaching retirement should take less risk than a young professional couple with a combined annual income of over $125,000. Younger people can afford to seek growth and take more risk because they can buy and hold for a longer time and also because they can anticipate a longer period of generating (probably rising) income. The preretirement couple may want some growth, but they also need safety. They'd be aghast to see the value of their portfolio drop 20 percent a few years before they retire.

CHAPTER **14**

New Developments

There were 3,000 mutual funds with $1 trillion in assets when I started writing this book. Now there are 4,000 funds with almost $2 trillion in assets. Needless to say, the fund business is booming.

Banks, insurance companies, and brokerage firms are getting into the business in a big way. New products are launched daily, and investors have a wide, but often confusing, array of investments to pick from.

BANKS SELL MUTUAL FUNDS

Your local depository institution may now offer a choice of brand name mutual funds or its own mutual products. More than $30 billion is now invested through mutual funds. However, you may pay extra fees for the convenience of investing at your bank. In addition to paying any loads, 12b-1 fees, and management fees, you may pay your friendly banker an administration fee or a small commission.

So if you plan to invest in mutual funds, you could save some money if you do it directly with the fund.

YOU DON'T NEED A WRAP ACCOUNT

The latest rage on Wall Street is the "wrap account." You can have your mutual funds managed by a professional money manager for a 2 percent to 3 percent annual fee. Your friendly stockbroker will evaluate your financial needs, goals, and tolerance for risk and find a mix of funds that fits your profile.

Avoid wrap accounts like the plague. Why pay someone as much as 2 percent to 3 percent a year to manage your mutual funds when you can do it yourself? Mutual fund groups like Stein Roe, Dreyfus, Fidelity Investments, and others have a free investment service to help you allocate your investments. Other fund groups publish newsletters with advice on how to split up your investment pie.

The lesson to be learned is this: Make your money work for you, not your stockbroker. Here are some free sources of information to help you make the right investment decisions.

Stein Roe & Farnham, a Chicago-based mutual fund group, just published a free investment strategies guide that's worth looking at. The guide shows you how much stocks, bonds, and Treasury bills have grown annually over the past 6 decades. You get an idea about what you can expect to earn over the longer term. The booklet tells you how to diversify based on five different investor profiles. For example, a moderate-growth investor should keep 5 percent in money funds, 15 percent in a government bond fund, 30 percent in an intermediate-term bond fund, and 50 percent in common stock funds. For a free copy of *How to Invest Wisely*, call 800-338-2550.

Porter Morgan, investment strategist with the Liberty Financial Companies, Boston, says retirees should not keep all their money in low-yielding certificates of deposits (CDs). The reason: People are living longer today, so they need to maintain their purchasing power by investing part of their money in common stock funds. Historically, over the last 6 decades stocks have registered about a 6 percent annual return over inflation.

"Of all the investment options, only stocks have beaten inflation over time," says Morgan. "Every investor regardless of age should own common stocks."

Today's maturing investor can look forward to a long and healthy retirement. A 65-year-old American has a 56 percent chance of living an additional 15 years, and a 36 percent chance of living to age 85.

So how much should you invest in stock funds? Morgan says to follow this easy rule of thumb: Subtract your age from 100. What is left is how much you should invest in a well-diversified low-risk common stock fund or portfolio of funds. Using this rule, someone aged 65 would invest 35 percent in a stock fund and the rest in bond funds or cash.

GOOD DEALS AT CHARLES SCHWAB

Discount brokerage firms are getting into the mutual fund business, too. Charles Schwab, a San Francisco–based discount brokerage firm with hundreds of offices nationwide, enables investors to buy more than 90 no-load funds from no-load mutual fund companies. You can keep all your mutual funds in one account and pay no transaction fees if you invest with the following fund groups: Janus, INVESCO, Dreyfus, Founders, Cappiello-Rushmore, Stein Roe, and Berger. Schwab is expected to add to this deal.

If you have an individual retirement account (IRA) with Schwab, you also get a break. You don't pay an IRA maintenance fee, and you can invest in the same group of funds without paying a transaction fee, provided you have an account worth $10,000 or more.

At the time of this writing, Fidelity Investments' discount brokerage firm was implementing a plan similar to Schwab's. Once Fidelity jumps on the bandwagon, other discounters will do the same.

MUTUAL FUNDS AND INSURANCE COMPANIES JOIN HANDS

Over $57 billion is invested in variable annuity and variable life insurance products. Some $53 billion is in variable annuities, which are mutual funds wrapped in insurance products, while $4 billion is in life insurance that enables policyholders to invest their cash value in mutual funds.

Why the popularity? There are tax advantages to investing in annuities and life insurance. With annuities, your money grows tax deferred until withdrawn. Life insurance cash values are not taxed. Neither are the death benefits.

Consumers willing to assume short-term risk in return for long-term gains by investing in stocks and bonds want an alternative to the low-yielding fixed-income products on the market today. Insurance companies are paying just 5 percent on fixed-rate annuities. Life insurance policies are paying 7 percent at the time of this writing. That sounds good, but after paying commissions and all those insurance fees, you are lucky if you earn 5 percent.

VARIABLE ANNUITIES

Variable annuities are hot products these days. More than $22 billion has flowed into variable annuities over the past year for a couple of reasons: The Clinton administration announced plans to raise taxes, so tax-deferred investments, like annuities, are popular—your money can grow tax free until you reach age 85, the age at which most insurance companies require withdrawals.

Death Benefit Guarantees

Variable annuity death benefit guarantees also appeal to risk-averse investors. A variable annuity is an insurance contract that lets you invest in stock and bond mutual funds. The insurance part of the annuity is the death benefit guarantee. If you die, you are guaranteed that your beneficiaries receive the money you contributed or the current value of the annuity, whichever is higher.

Investment Options

You can make lump-sum or regular payments into an annuity, and the money can grow tax deferred. After age 59½, you can take a lump-sum distribution from the variable annuity or receive monthly payments for life by annuitizing the contract.

You have a lot of investment options when you buy a variable annuity. You can invest in money funds, U.S. and overseas stock and bond funds, precious metals funds, and real estate funds. In addition, you can switch among funds or diversify your investments without having to pay capital gains taxes on the transactions. By contrast, every time you buy or sell a fund in a taxable account and make a profit, Uncle Sam collects his due.

Variable annuities have become even more enticing lately because a few no-load mutual fund companies are teaming up with insurance companies to offer lower-cost variable annuities.

High Fees

Before you rush out to stash a bundle of money in a variable annuity, you need to shop around. If you buy the wrong product, you can get stung by high annual fees and redemption charges.

Regardless of the annuity's fee structure, you must pay Uncle Sam if you redeem annuity proceeds early. A person under age 59½ would pay a 10 percent fine plus income taxes on the earnings portion of the annuity withdrawal.

Although your money grows tax free until withdrawal in an annuity, there is no free lunch. Variable annuities are high-cost products. According to *Morningstar's Variable Annuity/Life Performance Report*, you pay substantial fees when you invest. The average variable annuity hits you with a 2.26 percent annual charge, which is broken down as follows: a 1.26 percent annual mortality and expense charge; a 0.75 percent mutual fund expense charge; plus a $25 annual record and maintenance fee, which translates into another 0.25 percent charge on a $10,000 investment.

In addition to high annual fees, most annuities assess back-end surrender charges ranging from 5 percent to 9 percent. Each year the surrender charge drops 1 percent until it's diminished. Some contracts permit partial withdrawals of up to 10 percent of the value of the contract or 10 percent of the principal. However, you are typically charged the lesser of $25 or 2 percent of the amount withdrawn for that privilege.

Why the high cost? The mortality and expense charges are a source of revenue for the insurance company. The chances of the insurance company having to pay off on a death benefit are estimated to be less than one in one thousand. In addition, brokers and financial planners are paid commissions of up to 6 percent out of the mortality and expense charges. Higher fund management fees are a source of revenue to the fund companies. Back-end surrender charges also are used to compensate agents and financial planners.

"When you add it all up, those charges can reduce your returns by 2 percent annually over the long term," says Charles DeRose, a financial adviser based in Winter Park, Florida. According to DeRose, "Most annuities also lack liquidity. Each additional contribution you make is subject to its own surrender charge. If you make annual contributions into the annuity, you will never be able to escape the back-end loads."

The impact of annuity expenses is considerable. For example, in a worst-case scenario in which an annuity is surrendered by someone under age 59½, the investor would lose substantial income. Assuming that a $10,000 variable annuity grew at an annual rate of 8 percent over 8 years, the annuitant would receive just $13,577. That figure is based on 2 percent annual annuity fees, a 1 percent surrender charge, a 10 percent IRS fine, and a 28 percent income tax on the annuity's earnings. So, in actuality, the money would realize an annual return of just 3.9 percent over the 8 years.

"The expenses on most annuities are so high that they mitigate the tax-deferral benefits," adds DeRose. "And if you are unhappy with the performance of the annuity's funds, you are stuck with them unless you are willing to pay the withdrawal fees."

The Best Deals

Fortunately, there are a couple of low-cost variable annuity products on the market. The Vanguard Group of Investment Companies' Variable Annuity Plan and the Scudder Group of Mutual Funds' Horizon Plan are sold directly to investors. These two no-load fund groups can reduce their insurance charges and eliminate surrender fees because they don't pay sales commissions to brokers and financial planners.

Scudder's Horizon Plan/Charter National Life Insurance Co. (800-225-2470) has a variable annuity product, with total assets of $150 million, that offers annuitants a choice of five equity funds, two fixed-income funds, and a fixed-rate account. There is no surrender charge or maintenance fee. Depending on the fund, annuitants pay just 1.36 percent in total annuity charges, which includes a 0.70 percent mortality and expense charge and an average 0.66 percent fund management fee. For the U.S. equity, bond, and money funds, the fund management fee is 0.63 percent. You'll pay more, though, if you invest in the international stock fund, which has a management fee of 1.31 percent.

The Vanguard's Variable Annuity Plan/National Home Life Assurance Co. (800-622-7447), with assets of $500 million, offers investors a money fund, a balanced fund, and a bond or equity index fund. Mortality and expense charges are 0.55 percent, and management fees range from 0.32 percent to 0.42 percent. Depending on the fund, the total cost of the annuity ranges from 0.87 percent for the equity or bond index funds to 0.97 percent for the balanced fund. The total cost for the money fund is 0.55 percent. There is also a $25 annual maintenance charge, which translates into an additional 0.25 percent expense on a $10,000 investment.

When you invest in a Vanguard or Scudder variable annuity fund, you will not get a top performer or hot fund. What you get is good management and consistency. This is your retirement money. You want a fund or funds that give you the best return with the least amount of risk based on your comfort level.

Let's look at the returns, which are net of fees and charges according to Morningstar, Inc., data for the period ending in March 1993.

Scudder

The Scudder stable of funds includes:

• *The Scudder Horizon Plan Diversified Fund.*   This is a balanced fund that invests in both stocks and bonds. The fund gained 11.5 percent annually over the past 3 years.

• *The Scudder Horizon Plan International Fund.*   This is a stock fund that invests overseas. The fund gained just 1.75 percent annually over the past 3 years. But over 1 year ending in May, 1993, it was up 9.8 percent because of the surge in the world's stock markets.

• *The Scudder Horizon Plan Managed Bond Fund.* This is a longer-term bond fund. The fund gained 12 percent annually over the past 3 years. Now that interest rates are lower, however, the fund is up 4.5 percent year-to-date.

• *The Scudder Horizon Plan Money Market Fund.* This is a money fund that maintains a $1 per share net asset value. Over the past year the fund is up 2.3 percent.

Vanguard

The Vanguard stable of funds includes:

• *Vanguard Variable Annuity Plan Balanced Fund.* This is a balanced fund that invests in both stocks and bonds. The fund is up 14.5 percent since its inception 1 year ago.

• *Vanguard Variable Annuity Plan Equity Index.*   This is a growth-and-income fund that invests in the S&P 500. The fund is up 14.3 percent since its inception 1 year ago.

• *Vanguard Variable Annuity Plan High-Grade Bond Fund.*   This high-grade bond fund is up 11.9 percent since its inception 1 year ago.

• *Vanguard Variable Annuity Plan Money Market Fund.* This money fund has returned 2.8 percent since its inception 1 year ago.

No Free Lunch

Although the Vanguard and Scudder products cost investors about half as much as other annuities, even these surrender-charge-free products are not for everyone. Experts still say you should fund your IRA or 401(k) company pension plan before you consider an annuity.

"Annuities sold by no-load fund companies are expensive," says Jonathan Pond, author of the *New Century Family Money Book* (New York: Dell). "It's costly when you are charged 1 percent or more a year and your money is invested in a bond or money fund. You must be willing to assume greater risk and invest in a stock fund to reduce the impact of fees on the returns."

VARIABLE LIFE INSURANCE

Variable life (VL) insurance is like whole life insurance with a twist: You can buy life insurance and invest the cash value in common stock and bond funds. By contrast, with traditional whole life insurance you earn fixed dividend rates.

Life insurance is a tax-advantaged product. The nice thing about variable life is that your money grows tax free. You can also borrow against the cash value at low rates free and clear of taxes. Nor do your beneficiaries pay taxes on the death benefits.

Consult with your attorney, however, if you have an estate of more than $600,000. Your life insurance benefits are considered part of your taxable estate. So you need to do some estate planning.

Most VL insurance policies require you to pay annual insurance premiums. However, universal VL enables you to vary your premium payments. You can pay premiums for a few years, then cut back if you have a lot of other expenses. Later on, you can increase your payments. Be advised, however, that you can't overfund your universal VL policy. Your insurance agent or financial planner will review the premium payment rules. Depending on your coverage, there is a maximum annual premium payment that you can't exceed during the first 7 years you own the policy. If you pay in more than the limit, you could be subject to income taxes when you borrow or withdraw cash from your policy.

How to Pick an Insurance Policy

You buy life insurance for permanent income protection for your loved ones in case you are not around. Although your variable life insurance policy can be a valuable estate-planning instrument, it has its drawbacks. Insurance is a high-cost product. So shop around and compare policies.

The first step in finding the right policy is to check the insurance company's financial strength ratings. Firms rated A++ by A.M. Best, and triple A in claims-paying ability by Standard & Poor's, Moody's Investors Services, and Duff & Phelps are the safest.

You can obtain insurance company ratings by calling A.M. Best at 908-439-2200. The firm charges $2.50 per minute for your call. You can get free ratings from Standard & Poor's (212-208-1527), Moody's (212-553-0377), and Duff & Phelps (312-368-3157).

After you've put together a list of safe outfits, it's important to compare your policy costs.

Here are the charges you run up against when you buy life insurance:

• You may pay a sales commission of as much as 50 percent in the first year of your policy. So if you purchased a cash-value product and paid for the insurance component, less than half of your premium is invested in the cash-value account of the policy. In addition, depending on the insurance company, you may pay, on average, about a 3 percent annual commission over the life of the policy.

• Depending on the company, you pay about $100 a year in policy fees and administrative charges.

• You will pay mortality charges. It may cost middle-aged policyholders as much as $100 per $1,000 of coverage.

• If you liquidate your policy in the first 10 years, you'll pay a back-end surrender charge. Surrender charges vary from company to company. However, if you cash out just a few years after you bought the policy, you lose almost 100 percent of your money.

How do you evaluate the impact of all those fees on your policy? Consumer advocates recommend that you ask your insurance agent for the internal rate of return (IRR) on your policy. The IRR shows you the rate of return on your cash value less all the fees and charges. Although the insurance company may be crediting you with 7 percent or 8 percent on your cash value, net of expenses, you may be earning 5 percent or 6 percent, depending on the amount of annual premium paid.

It's also important to look at the interest-adjusted cost-surrender index. This index is listed at the end of your insurance policy's illustration. It evaluates the cost per thousand dollars of insurance coverage. The lower the index, the lower the cost of the insurance.

NO-LOAD, LOW-COST INVESTING

Today, you can invest in a wide variety of no-load mutual funds. There are 2,000 commission-free funds to pick from. A few years ago, there were half as many. Furthermore, the no-loads perform as well as or better than load funds.

Last year investors paid almost $6 billion in commissions to purchase stock and bond funds. That money represents a tremendous amount of lost income over the years. Assuming that the $6 billion in commissions would earn just 5 percent annually over the next 10 years, the lost income would have grown to $9.77 billion. That translates into an estimated future loss of $2,443 for every stock and bond fund shareholder today.

"You will be a lot wealthier if you invest in no-load mutual funds," says Sheldon Jacobs, publisher of the *No Load Fund Investor*, a mutual fund newsletter published in Irvington-on-Hudson, New York. "Most load funds hit you with a 12b-1 sales distribution fee and 4.5 to 6.5 percent front-end commission. Others may have no front-end load, but you pay a 12b-1 and or a back-end charge. Some funds have a combination of charges or have deferred sales charges that decline to zero over a few years."

Every investor pays the fund company a fee to invest and manage securities. Management fees are annual charges against total assets in the fund that range as low as 25 basis points or 0.25 percent for bond funds to 1 percent for equity funds.

Every investor also pays for fund operating and administrative expenses. These expenses are deducted from the fund's asset value. That's why the price of a fund is referred to as the net asset value.

After management fees and expenses, you may or may not incur other charges. No-load funds are commission free. Load funds may charge a front-end or back-end load or deferred sales charges. Both load and no-load funds may also charge you a 12b-1 distribution fee.

Jacobs points out that the lost income from paying load fees and other charges can mount up over the years. Assuming you invest $1,000 a year in a fund with a 5 percent load, it would cost you $50 per $1,000 invested. If you invested the money at 8 percent over 10 years, the load fund would grow to $1,954, compared with $2,159 in a no-load fund.

Even if you invest in no-load funds, you lose income from paying a 12b-1 sales distribution fee. Irving Strauss, president of the 100 percent No Load Mutual Fund Council in New York, says that the 12b-1 fee, which is used to pay for advertising and promotion expenses, increases the cost of investing and cuts a fund's performance.

"A $10,000 investment in a no-load fund that earns 10 percent annually will grow to $25,937 over 10 years," says Strauss. "If a 1 percent 12b-1 fee is deducted from the fund, the money grows to $23,674. You are short-changed $2,263 when you invest in the 12b-1 fund."

Strauss says that the easiest way to compare funds with 12b-1 charges is to look at the equivalent front-end load charge.

"The American Association of Individual Investors, Chicago, has published a table that shows that long-term investors pay a lot in 12b-1 charges," says Strauss. "Paying an annual .25 percent 12b-1 fee over 10 years is the same as paying a 2.5 percent front-end load. If you hold the fund for 20 years, it's the same as paying a five percent load. A .50 percent 12b-1 fee is equal to a five percent front-end load if you invest in the fund for 10 years. Over

20 years, it's the same as paying a 10 percent front-end load."

Don Phillips, publisher of *Morningstar Mutual Funds*, stresses that if a stockbroker or financial planner tells you that no-load funds have higher expenses than load funds, "Don't believe them."

A Morningstar, Inc., analysis confirms exactly the opposite. Pure no-load funds have lower average expense ratios (ER) and register higher returns than funds with higher expenses. For example: The average ER for 643 pure no-load stock and bond funds in the June 1992 study was 0.97 percent. The average ER for 188 no-loads with 12b-1 fees was 1.48 percent. The average ER for 1,509 other funds was 1.32 percent.

"Low expenses translate into higher returns for investors," says Phillips. "Not only do no-load funds cost less to purchase, but they are cheaper to hold. The idea that no-load funds have higher expenses is simply not true. Pure no-load funds pass on the benefits of rising assets to a far greater degree than load funds."

Also avoid the new dual-priced mutual funds. Dual-priced funds have A and B class shares. The class A shares have a front-end load but no 12b-1 charge. The class B shares have no up-front sales charges but carry a disappearing 12b-1 fee and a deferred sales charge.

A and B class shares are a marketing gimmick to make it look like you are getting a good deal.

Another way to save is to avoid funds with high fund expense ratios. That's a number that shows the relationship of fund expenses to the fund's net asset value. High expenses eat into returns. If you invested $10,000 in a stock fund and earned 10 percent a year, your money would grow to $13,674, assuming the fund sported a 1 percent expense ratio, which is the industry average, according to the *Mutual Fund Forecaster*, published in Fort Lauderdale, Florida. By contrast, if the same fund had an above-average expense ratio of 1.8 percent, the money would grow to $11,992 over the same time period, representing $1,682 in lost income.

"Far too many investors ignore annual expenses and focus on sales and redemption fees," says Norm Fosback, publisher of the *Mutual Fund Forecaster*. "Sales and redemption charges are one-time charges. Expenses go on year after year. For long-term holding periods, expenses are a greater burden than sales charges. For example, 10 consecutive years of bearing two percent annual expense charges is about twice as expensive as a one-time 9.3 percent sales load coupled with a two-tenths of one percent expense charges."

Fixed-income investors also can save a bundle. William E. Donoghue, publisher of *Donoghue's Moneyletter*, Ashland, Massachusetts, says you can make an extra one-quarter of 1 percent if you invest in money funds that are absorbing expenses. That amounts to earning $25 more on every $1,000 you invest over 1 year. Some fund groups that absorb expenses on some of their money funds include Dreyfus, Fidelity Spartan, and the Strong Group, Donoghue adds.

In addition to load charges, 12b-1 fees, and high expense ratios, unnecessary taxes on the purchase and sale of fund shares serve to cut your returns.

Jacobs says you should avoid buying a fund before it distributes capital gains or dividends. Even though you just bought into a fund, you are required by law to pay tax on capital gains and dividend distributions that the fund has accumulated for the year.

"Check before you invest, because any shareholder of record before what is called the ex.-

dividend date, will receive and pay taxes on the distributions," Jacobs stresses.

Gerald Perritt, publisher of the *Mutual Fund Letter*, Chicago, also says that investors can slash the tax paid on mutual fund distributions by investing in funds that buy and hold stocks for a longer term.

"Look for a fund which will pay minimum distributions," says Perritt. "Over the years I have observed that funds with high portfolio turnover tend to pay higher distributions. Funds that frequently turn over portfolios build up large annual capital gains which must be distributed to shareholders. Low-turnover funds take fewer profits during the year and avoid making distributions."

Among the low-turnover stock funds that Perritt favors are the Dodge & Cox Stock Fund, Fidelity Congress Fund, T. Rowe Price New Era Fund, and Vanguard's Wellington, Windsor, and Index 500 funds.

BE ALERT TO CAPITAL GAINS TAXES

Investors should also avoid the IRS's *wash sale* rules when they buy and sell fund shares.

For example, you might want to sell mutual fund shares at a loss so you can write them off on your income taxes. But if the fund is a good long-term investment, you might want to buy them back later. To qualify for a tax write-off, however, you have to stay clear of a wash sale. You can't repurchase your stock for 31 calendar days after you sell it. You can't be a front-runner either. You can't buy more stock in the same firm up to 30 days before the planned tax-loss sale. Otherwise, the IRS won't let you write off the loss on your income taxes.

Jullian Block, author of *Year-Round Tax Strategies* (Prima Publications, Rocklin, CA), says the wash

wash sale: sale of an investment to gain a tax write-off followed within 31 days by a repurchase of the same investment

sale rule prevents savvy investors from paying their fair share of income taxes. If investors unloaded losers, wrote off the loss on their taxes, and bought the stock back right away, they would be abusing the tax laws. However, Block says, there are several ways to avoid wash sale rules and profit. For example:

• Sell the fund shares at a loss, wait 31 days, and buy them back. The sale at a loss can occur at the close of trading on the last business day of the year. For example, say you sell at a loss on October 28. You can't write off the loss unless you buy back the stock 31 days later on November 27. The advantage: You get a tax deduction and don't have to put money back into the market. The drawback: You will lose the tax savings if the mutual fund price goes up in the 31 days before the repurchase of the security.

• Buy and then sell. Block says to buy the same amount of mutual fund shares you already own, wait at least 31 days to avoid the wash sale rule, and then sell the original holding. You use this tactic until the end of November, so you can sell at the end of the year. Suppose your mutual fund or stock is down 10 percent in value but you think it's a good long-term investment. Your accountant says you need the write-off. So you avoid the wash sale by buying more shares at least 31 days before you sell your original shares at a loss. The drawback: You are doubling up on your investment. If the stock plunges, you double your losses. The advantage: If you believe the investment will move up, this is an excellent way to enhance your return.

• Switch investments. You can avoid the wash sale rule if you buy a stock in the same industry. Say your ABC mutual fund is down 10 percent and XYZ mutual fund has a positive earnings outlook.

You sell your shares in ABC at a loss and buy XYZ. The drawback: You may be giving up dividend income. In addition, the ABC company may be more profitable over the long haul than XYZ.

Block cautions investors to check the transaction costs of buying and selling stock before attempting to get a write-off. The cost of the transactions may outweigh the tax savings.

THE ADVANTAGES OF CONSOLIDATION

If you have mutual fund IRAs with holdings in several fund families, you can save on your annual retirement savings maintenance charges. Most mutual fund groups charge you $10 per year per fund in your IRA account. If you own four or five mutual funds, it will cost you $50 a year. However, by consolidating your mutual fund with a discount broker like Charles Schwab, you can save a bundle. After paying the initial opening fee of $18, Schwab charges you just .6 percent of principal for an investment of $15,000 or less. So if you contribute $4,000 a year into a joint IRA, for example, it will cost you $26.40 a year, or $23.60 less than keeping five funds with different mutual fund families.

In addition, the discount broker will eliminate transaction fees on selected funds of several no-load groups including Janus, Founders, Financial, Berger, Dreyfus, Federated, Nueberger Berman, Schwab, and Stein Roe.

HAVE A FINANCIAL GAME PLAN

You can't invest without considering your estate. Although estate planning is beyond the scope of this book, it is important to review some essentials.

You must have some type of estate game plan to make sure your loved ones have income protection and inherit your property.

First, you need to have a will. If you have a sizable estate, you may need a trust. Regardless of your age, marital status, or health, you need a will to protect your assets. If you die intestate, without a will, you are putting the state in charge of deciding who gets what. That means that you may accidentally disinherit a family member or close friend. And if you and your spouse die without leaving specific instructions for the guardianship of your children, you give up the right to decide who will raise them. Plus, dying without a will may commit your estate to a long and expensive wait in probate court.

Second, problems can pop up if your estate isn't well organized. For instance, your house, bank accounts, stocks, and any other personal property that may be owned jointly (this is called joint tenancy) will transfer to your spouse by law, regardless of what your will says. And in many states, if you are married and have children, if you die intestate your spouse may inherit only a portion of your estate while the rest would be distributed equally to your children.

Other assets such as life insurance proceeds and pension benefits pass to named beneficiaries unless you specify an estate or trust as a beneficiary. Because some assets don't pass exclusively by a will, it is especially important that titles on property and other personal holdings match those named in your will to avoid complications.

Going One Step Beyond a Will

Today many people are using trusts instead of wills. A trust, attorneys say, is more flexible than a will.

A trust, like a will, is a written legal document. It enables you to have your money and other assets managed by a *trustee* so that your heirs will receive your assets when you die.

trustee: a person or organization that holds property for you when you sign a trust agreement

"Establishing a trust could be an important part of estate planning," says Arlene Harris, an attorney with Shea & Gould, New York. "Some types of trusts enable you to save money by forgoing probate and let you leave money directly to your heirs. Other kinds of trusts are used for estate tax planning. You can reduce your estate taxes and provide income to your spouse or children. However, these goals also can be accomplished by a will, and a living trust is not necessarily the right advice."

Trust and estate-tax laws are complex. So before you act, Harris advises, consumers should seek the advice of an experienced attorney who specializes in trusts and estates.

For more information on estate planning, write the American Association of Retired Persons at 1909 K Street, NW, Washington, DC 20049. Also contact your state's bar association for a list of lawyers who specialize in estate planning.

There are two kinds of trusts you can use. A testamentary trust is created within a will and takes effect when you die. A living trust, or inter vivos trust, operates when you are alive.

A trust can be set up as either revocable or irrevocable.

A revocable living trust gives you a lot of flexibility. You control a revocable living trust and can change the terms of the trust at any time. You can manage the assets, or you can hire someone to manage the money based on the trust's instructions. In addition, you can distribute the assets in the trust to your loved ones, or you can keep the money in the trust for as long as you want. With a revocable living trust, you can avoid the costly process of probate, which, depending on the size of the estate, can cost several thousand dollars.

Revocable living trusts do have drawbacks. For example:

• Trusts are expensive to set up. Depending on the attorney you hire, you can pay as little as $50 to $100 for a will, but it can cost over $1,000 for a living trust.

• Many states require you to have a cotrustee. That means dealing with another person.

• Not all of your assets can be put in a living trust. You can't get a mortgage from some Florida lenders if the home is included in a family or living trust. As a result, lawyers are forced to draw up a "pour-over" will, and your heirs must go through probate to inherit the property. In other states, you may have problems refinancing the house if it's in a family trust.

• Finally, although you avoid probate cost when you have a revocable living trust, the assets in the trust are considered part of your taxable estate.

By contrast, the terms of an irrevocable trust cannot be changed. A trustee manages and distributes the assets of the trust based on the trust document. You give up ownership of any asset you placed in this type of trust. Legally, the assets are considered gifts to your beneficiaries. However, Arlene Harris notes that there are limits to the tax advantages of irrevocable trusts. You may pay gift taxes when you make contributions to the trust.

Although you can't change the terms of an irrevocable trust, there are two important advantages to this legal document:

1. You avoid probate.
2. You reduce the estate-tax bite because assets in

the trust are not considered part of your taxable estate.

Testamentary trusts are a different ball game altogether. They are used in special situations. For example, say you want to establish a fund to pay for your grandchildren's education but feel they might squander the money. With a testamentary trust, you can see to it that they're taken care of. The will, containing instructions, goes to probate, and the trust is set up. A trustee then takes control of the assets. Assets in a testamentary trust are considered part of your taxable estate because you have had control of the money during your lifetime.

Keeping Your Estate from the Taxman

If you have a sizable estate of $600,000 or more, you need more than a will. Fail to meet with an attorney about estate-tax planning and your heirs may face estate taxes ranging from marginal tax rates of 37 percent to more than 55 percent. For example, your heirs will pay $55,600 in federal estate taxes on an estate that's worth $750,000. They will owe $1,098,000 on an estate worth $3 million.

Fortunately, there are a number of ways to reduce the estate-tax bill. Arlene Harris, of Shea & Gould, has several suggestions. Depending on your situation, here are some of the basic estate-tax-planning moves you can make:

• You can leave all your property to your spouse estate-tax free. This is known as taking a marital deduction. However, when the second spouse dies, estate taxes must be paid.
• You can give up to $600,000 to your children or others estate-tax free. Everyone gets a partial tax break on their estate. No one pays the first $197,800

of estate taxes due on assets worth $600,000. This is known as a unified tax credit.

• If you had a $1.2 million estate, you could give $600,000 to your spouse and $600,000 to your children or someone else estate-tax free. If you plan on giving money to your children, you can put the $600,000 into what is known as a by-pass trust. The spouse can then receive benefits from the trust and, if properly drawn, no estate tax is payable at either death.

If you leave all your property to your spouse, you escape the taxman. Eventually, however, estate taxes must be paid when the second spouse dies. Ruldolf Watz, a financial planner and director of insurance products with Value Line Securities Inc., New York, stresses that anyone with an estate exceeding $600,000 should consider setting up a life insurance irrevocable trust. The life insurance proceeds in the trust escape estate taxation, plus the death benefits can be used to pay the estate-tax bill.

"You can put an existing policy into an irrevocable life insurance trust or the trust can purchase a new policy on your life," says Watz. "When the first spouse dies, the death benefits can be used to pay the estate taxes."

Watz adds that if the bulk of your estate goes to your spouse, you probably won't need the life insurance proceeds until the death of the second spouse, when estate taxes are due. So you could establish a life insurance trust and purchase a second-to-die life insurance policy. Then you postpone paying taxes until the surviving spouse dies.

"You have to sit down with an experienced financial planner and attorney, and look at all your options," adds Watz. "They will estimate your estate's value, how much taxes may be due and whether you should buy a first-to-die or second-to-die policy."

Although there are benefits to using life insurance to pay taxes, there are pitfalls to consider. For example:

• For the irrevocable life insurance trust to be legal, you have to set up the trust as soon as possible. Lawyers say you have to transfer the insurance into the irrevocable trust at least 3 years before your death, otherwise the insurance proceeds are considered part of your taxable estate.

• If you are seriously ill, you may not qualify for life insurance.

• You have to do business with a financially sound insurance company. If an insurance company goes bankrupt, you may not get all your money right away. The safest companies carry A++ financial-strength ratings by A.M. Best and triple-A claims-paying ratings by Standard & Poor's, Moody's, and Duff and Phelps.

• Purchasing life insurance to pay future estate taxes can be expensive. Depending on your age, physical condition, and the size of your estate, you can purchase whole life or term insurance. Someone who bought $1 million of life insurance to meet a future tax liability may have to pay annual premiums of about $20,000 a year for a whole life policy. Term insurance costs less. However, as you get older, term insurance costs more than level premium whole life insurance. One solution is to combine term and whole life insurance and put them into a trust.

Two helpful sources of information on estate planning are *The Wall Street Journal Guide to Understanding Personal Finance* (New York: Lightbulb Press), and *The Handbook of Estate Planning*, by

Robert Esperti and Renno Peterson (New York: McGraw-Hill).

You Need Insurance Protection

Last but not least, you have to tie your investment game plan in with your insurance and retirement needs.

Financial planners say you need between five and eight times your current wages to protect your family when you are not around. Consult with a local insurance agent or financial planner about getting adequate coverage.

You also may need disability insurance coverage. In case you get injured, you should have coverage that pays you 60 percent of your current income. The policy should be noncancelable, annually renewable, and carry inflation protection.

You Need to Save for Retirement

retirement savings plan: a way of saving for your retirement by putting earned income into a tax-deductible individual retirement account (IRA), a company pension plan such as a 401(k) or, for the self-employed, a Keogh plan

If you work for a living, you need a *retirement savings plan*. If you don't have a company pension plan, start an individual retirement account (IRA). Single people can sock away $2,000 a year and get a tax deduction. Married couples who file a joint return can make a $4,000 annual tax-deductible contribution.

Even those with a company plan can make contributions. Singles and heads of households who earn between $25,000 and $35,000 lose about $1 in deductions for every $5 they contribute to an IRA. But no tax deductions are allowed if you earn more than $35,000.

Married couples who file joint returns get the full deduction if they earn under $40,000. Between $40,000 and $50,000, they lose about $1 in deductions for every $5 they contribute. You lose the deduction with earnings of more than $50,000.

Company 401(k) pension plans are also popular. You can put up to $8,000 a year into a company plan. The contribution limits are indexed to inflation, so next year it will be more. You also get a tax deduction. The amount you contribute reduces your taxable income. In addition, employers can make matching contributions, and your money is invested in your choice of mutual funds.

Conclusion

When you invest in mutual funds, or any type of investment, you have to look at the whole picture. Investing should be one part of a financial game plan that includes retirement, insurance, and estate planning. So before you invest, either meet with a financial adviser or do your homework and evaluate your needs and goals.

Glossary

adviser   an investment professional hired to provide investment advice and management to a mutual fund company

aggressive growth fund   a high-risk fund that invests for maximum capital appreciation

automatic investments   process of electronically debiting your checking account and automatically investing the money in the fund of your choice

balanced funds   funds that invest in both stocks and bonds, usually with a stock-to-bond ratio of 60:40 (Some funds also diversify among domestic and overseas securities.)

beta value   a statistical measure of risk that tells you how much a fund or security moves in relation to the market (The S&P 500 has a beta value of 1.)

bond credit ratings   a measure of a bond issuer's creditworthiness (Investment-grade bonds rated triple-A to single-A by Standard & Poor's and Moody's Investors Services are the safest. Low-rated or speculative bonds are considered junk bonds.)

broker dealers   companies that buy and sell fund shares to investors (Underwriters sell funds to broker dealers who in turn sell fund shares to investors.)

bond funds   mutual funds that invest in fixed-income securities (Funds are distinguished by the type of securities—government or corporate, domestic or foreign—in the portfolio, the average maturity of the securities, and the credit quality of the issuer.)

capital gains   the profit made when a fund manager sells securities in the portfolio; also the profit realized by the shareholder when fund shares are sold (When a fund realizes capital gains, the gains are distributed to the shareholders of the fund either in cash or reinvestment of new shares.)

capital appreciation   the profit made on an investment, i.e., the increase in the value of the fund shares over time

constant dollar investing   a method of investing whereby a portfolio is rebalanced after a specified period of time to a fixed dollar amount

constant ratio investing   a method of investing whereby a fixed percentage of the investment is maintained between stocks and bonds (e.g., 50 percent stocks and 50 percent bonds)

contingent deferred sales charge   a back-end redemption charge that declines to zero over a specified number of years, after which fund shares can be sold without paying a back-end load

custodian bank   a bank responsible for custody of fund shares, which are kept in a separate account from other assets

diversification   splitting your investments among different types of mutual funds to reduce risk, or choosing mutual funds that hold a large number of issuers in a wide variety of industries

dividend   short-term profits, stock dividends, or interest income distributed by mutual funds to shareholders in the form of cash or more shares

dollar cost averaging   making regular investments in a fund so that over time, the average cost of your investment will be more than the current market price when you sell

foreign currency risk   occurs when the market value of an investment changes with the value of the currency used to purchase a security

growth funds funds that invest in well-seasoned companies for long-term growth

growth-and-income funds funds that invest for both capital appreciation and income

income funds funds that invest in high-dividend-paying stocks

investment company another name for a mutual fund company

investment objectives a description of a fund's investment plan (Stock funds that invest for growth look for capital appreciation. Some funds invest for both growth and income. Other funds preserve capital by investing in both stocks and bonds. Fixed-income funds invest for safety, liquidity, or yield.)

load a sales charge that can range from 2 percent to 8.5 percent; may be paid at time of purchase (front-end load) or when fund is sold (back-end load)

management fees fees a fund pays to its investment adviser

money market mutual funds funds that invest in short-term money market instruments such as Treasury bills

municipal bonds funds that invest in tax-free bonds issued by state and local governments

net asset value (NAV) price of the fund per share net of fund expenses (Funds with sales loads have two share prices—the offering price, which reflects NAV plus sales charges, and the redemption price, which is the NAV the broker charges to buy back the shares.)

no-load mutual fund a fund free of sales charges

overseas mutual funds funds that invest in stocks or bonds in foreign countries (Global funds invest both here and abroad; international funds invest strictly overseas.)

precious metals mutual funds funds that own gold and mining stocks; may also invest in related metals and mining operations

prospectus   the legal document that investors are required to read before they invest to learn important information about investment objectives, risks, fees, and the fund's management

retirement savings plan   a way of saving for your retirement by putting earned income into a tax-deductible individual retirement account (IRA), a company pension plan such as a 401(k) or, for the self-employed, a Keogh plan

risk   factors such as inflation, rising interest rates, defaults by bond issuers, poor financial performance by a company, or downward movements in the financial markets that may cause stock or bond prices to drop

sales distribution fees   annual fees that can range from 0.25 percent to 1 percent of total assets in fund and are used to pay for promotion and distribution of fund shares (also known as a 12b-1 fees)

sector funds   funds that invest in specific industries such as utilities, chemicals, or technology

Securities and Exchange Commission   the U.S. government agency that regulates mutual fund or investment companies under the Investment Company Act of 1940

small-company stock funds   funds that invest in stocks sold on the over-the-counter stock market

standard deviation   the margin of error in a statistical forecast

systematic withdrawals   a fixed percentage of fund assets paid out to investors who primarily want additional income

tax-free bond fund   fund that invests in municipal bonds (Shareholders don't pay federal income taxes on municipal bond interest income. Investors in single-state municipal bond funds don't pay local, state, or federal taxes on the interest income from a municipal bond fund.)

transfer agent   a company hired by the mutual fund to keep shareholder account records

trustee a person or organization that holds property for you when you sign a trust agreement

12b-1 fees marketing distribution fees, ranging from 0.25 percent to 0.5 percent of assets, that shareholders pay annually

value investing when a fund buys underpriced stocks that have the potential to perform well

value averaging a variation of dollar cost averaging that calls for increasing dollar contributions

value ratio investing an investment tactic whereby money is invested in aggressive stock funds when the stock market is considered undervalued and in conservative funds when the market is overvalued

wash sale sale of an investment to gain a tax write-off followed within 31 days by a repurchase of the same investment

Sources of Information

MUTUAL FUND NEWSLETTERS

Donoghue's Moneyletter
290 Eliot Street
P.O. Box 91004
Ashland, MA 01721

Mutual Fund Forecaster
3471 North Federal Highway
Fort Lauderdale, FL 33306

Income & Safety
3471 North Federal Highway
Fort Lauderdale, FL 33306

The No Load Fund X
DAL Investment Company
235 Montgomery Street
San Francisco, CA 94104

The No Load Investor
P.O. Box 283
Irvington-on-Hudson, NY 10706

The Mutual Fund Letter
Investment Information Services,
  Inc.
680 North Lake Shore Drive,
  Suite 2038
Chicago, IL 60611

*Jay Schabacker's Mutual Fund
  Investing*
7811 Montrose Road
Potomac, MD 20854

L/G No Load Mutual Fund Analyst
300 Montgomery Street
San Francisco, CA 94104

United Mutual Fund Selector
Babson United Building
107 Prescott Street
Wellesley Hills, MA 02181

MUTUAL FUND PERFORMANCE REPORTS

CDA/Wiesenberger
1355 Piccard Drive
Rockville, MD 20850

Donoghue's Mutual Fund Almanac
290 Eliot Street
P.O. Box 91004
Ashland, MA 01721

Handbook For No Load Investors
P.O. Box 283
Irvington-on-Hudson, NY 10706

*Lipper Mutual Fund Performance
   Analysis*
Lipper Analytical Services
74 Trinity Place
New York, NY 10006

5 Star Investor and *Morningstar
   Mutual Funds*
53 West Jacson Street, Suite 352
Chicago, IL 60604

Mutual Fund Encyclopedia
Investment Information Services,
   Inc.
680 N. Lake Shore Drive, Suite
   2038
Chicago, IL 60611

BOOKS

Diversify: Investors Guide to Asset Allocation Strategies, by Alan Lavine and Gerald Perritt (Chicago: Dearborn Financial Publishing, Inc., 1990).

William E. Donoghue's No Load Mutual Fund Guide, by William E. Donoghue (New York: Harper & Row, 1983).

William E. Donoghue's Complete Money Market Guide, by William E. Donoghue (New York: Harper & Row, 1982).

Mutual Fund Fact Book (Washington, DC: Investment Company Institute, 1993).

The Individual Investors Guide To No Load Mutual Funds (Chicago: American Association of Individual Investors, 1993).

Index

0-595-26892-7